BASIS OF AMERICAN HISTORY
1500 — 1900

AMERICAN CLASSICS

BASIS OF
AMERICAN HISTORY
1500 – 1900

Livingston Farrand

FREDERICK UNGAR PUBLISHING CO.
NEW YORK

Republished 1964 in the
AMERICAN CLASSICS SERIES

First published 1904

Printed in the United States of America

Library of Congress Catalog Card No. 64-25548

CONTENTS

MAPS

AUTHOR'S PREFACE

THE present work is an attempt to describe, as fully as the limits of the book will permit, those features of North America and its native inhabitants which have been of greatest significance in the history of the United States. For the physical features of the continent, numerous trustworthy works are available; for the fauna and flora there are various general treatises of value; while for the aborigines there is not a single comprehensive book of a satisfactory character. This lack has long been a source of embarrassment to students of American ethnology, and for that reason the chief emphasis in the following pages is laid upon the distribution and the culture of the Indians.

The difficulties to be overcome in the preparation of a general descriptive account of the Indian tribes are not caused by lack of material. The systematic researches of the Bureau of American Ethnology in Washington, and of such institutions as the Peabody Museum of Harvard, the American Museum of Natural History in New York, and the Field-Columbian Museum of Chicago, added to the accumulated products of individual writers, afford an enormous

mass of available information.   The task of the present volume, therefore, has been one of condensation.
Of many omissions, ruthless but necessary, I am
fully conscious and equally regretful.   It is my hope,
however, that the book may prove of some service
as an introduction to the study of American ethnology as well as to that of American history.

I am grateful for this opportunity of acknowledg-
ing my deep and constant obligation to my friend
and colleague Franz Boas, whose extraordinary an-
thropological learning and enthusiasm have been to
me for years a source of inspiration, and whose
judgment has been always at my disposal in the
preparation of this volume.   I wish also to acknowl-
edge particularly the assistance of Mr. A. B. Lewis,
who has co-operated at every stage of the work; and
of Dr. J. F. McGregor and Mr. C. B. Robinson, who
gave indispensable aid in the treatment of topics
with which they were especially familiar.

LIVINGSTON FARRAND.

BASIS OF AMERICAN HISTORY

BASIS OF AMERICAN HISTORY

CHAPTER I

GENERAL PHYSIOGRAPHY OF NORTH AMERICA
(1500–1900)

THAT the economic conditions of any people will be largely determined by their physical environment is particularly true in the earlier development of a territory, before the increase and overcrowding of population through commerce and manufacture force an artificial adaptation to changed conditions. Environment also reacts upon the physical and mental constitution of the inhabitants and modifies and determines their culture. The industrial life of the Eskimo of the arctic is sharply contrasted with that of the desert dwellers of Arizona and New Mexico; and the less tangible differences of temperament and mental character of the two groups are likewise to a large degree due to the variations of climate and soil. The contour of the land, by favoring or forbidding

3

migration and the consequent contact of differing groups, also affects development of culture even among primitive peoples whose institutions tend to evolve along independent lines. Hence the political fortunes even of a people of high culture are largely dependent upon the physical geography of their home.

A comprehensive history of the American nation must, therefore, be based upon an accurate appreciation of the features of the territory within which it is working out its future; and the physical geography of the United States demands consideration not only of that portion embraced within the present political boundaries, but also of the general characteristics of the continent of North America as a whole.[1]

The great triangle of North America presents its base to the arctic and narrows to its apex in the tropics. This means that its greater area is included in high latitudes and ruled by a relatively severe climate. While the United States lies mainly in the southern half, roughly between the parallels of 29° N. and 49° N., its greatest extent lies far enough north to gain the advantage which colder climates seem to possess in producing efficient racial groups.

The character of the coast - line of a continent is a matter of prime concern in colonization or invasion, and becomes of constantly greater im-

[1] For general authorities on the physiography of the United States, see chap. xviii., below.

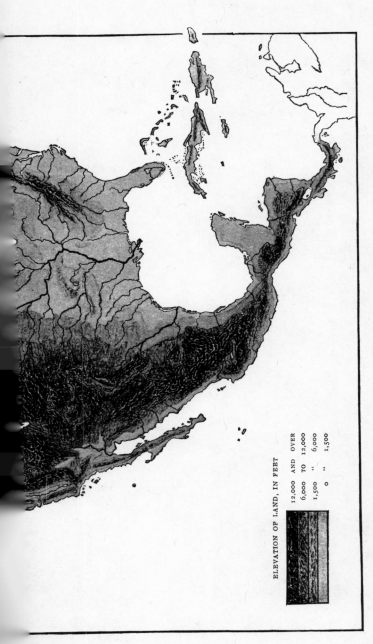

ELEVATION OF LAND, IN FEET

12,000 AND OVER
6,000 TO 12,000
1,500 " 6,000
0 " 1,500

RELIEF MAP OF NORTH AMERICA

portance with the development of civilization and
the growth of commerce.   Hence the discussion of
that coast is a convenient avenue of approach to
the task of this volume.   In general, the North
American coast is irregular and broken, especially
on the Atlantic shore.   Deep bays and consequent
peninsulas are common; yet of Labrador, Nova
Scotia, Florida, Yucatan, Lower California, and
Alaska, only Nova Scotia and Florida have lain
within the main tracks of conquest and immigration.
Yucatan is of interest chiefly as the seat of a remarkable native culture in pre-Columbian times;
Labrador and Lower California have always remained little more than names upon the map; and
Alaska is just beginning to play a part in history.

The indentations of the coast are of far greater
historical importance.   Hudson Bay, the Gulf of
St. Lawrence, the Bay of Fundy, Massachusetts
Bay, Buzzards Bay, Long Island Sound, Delaware
and Chesapeake bays, Albemarle and Pamlico
sounds, and the Gulf of Mexico with its branches,
represent the great breaks of the Atlantic coast-
line; while, in contrast, the Gulf of California and
Puget Sound are the only considerable interruptions
of the Pacific shore.   The same difference marks the
smaller bays and harbors.   At frequent intervals
along its stretch the Atlantic coast offers admirable
protection for shipping; while on the entire Pacific
coast of the United States there are practically but
two natural harbors, that of San Francisco and the

reaches of Puget Sound. The harbor of San Diego, near the southern line of California, though it affords a certain degree of shelter, is as yet of minor importance; and the mouth of the Columbia River is admirably situated for commerce, but the shallowness of its waters and the great bar at the entrance have thus far rendered it impracticable for vessels of deep draught.

North of the United States boundary, on the Pacific, British Columbia and a large part of Alaska abut upon a fiord coast; outlying islands and deep, narrow, cliff-bordered inlets make good harbors, but the adjacent interior is undeveloped and forbidding. A somewhat similar fiord coast is found on the Atlantic side, along the Canadian provinces and, to a greater extent, in Maine. The indentations of Maine, while comparatively shallow, offer in many cases excellent harbors.

Massachusetts Bay, formed by the projection of Cape Cod, contains Boston Harbor, and the hospitality of the coast increases as one progresses southward. Narragansett and Buzzards bays are succeeded by the shores of Long Island Sound, with many small, protected havens, until at New York an extraordinary combination of unrivalled natural advantages makes that point the most important centre of commerce on the continent. The depth of water, the strikingly favorable arrangement of the land about the mouth of the Hudson River, and the fact that the Hudson is the commercial gateway to the interior, have conspired to place New York beyond competition in the development of Atlantic ports.

Delaware Bay is the estuary of the Delaware River; and Chesapeake Bay, still farther south, receives the Susquehanna, the Potomac, and the James. Neither bay compares as a harbor with New York, but they have been of great moment, nevertheless, in the early and later history of America. From the Chesapeake southward to the extremity of Florida the indentations are fewer, smaller, and shallower, but are of great historical importance. The Gulf of Mexico is notable not only as the receiver of the Mississippi drainage, but as an element in modifying the climate of the country by its situation and by the ocean currents to which it gives rise.

Of superlative importance not only as barriers to the spread of population, but also as influences modifying climatic conditions, are the mountain-ranges of a continent. In North America the most striking relief feature is the so - called Cordillera, an immense mountain chain stretching along the western area from Central America to Alaska. In reality it is a great plateau with a breadth of one thousand miles in the United States and with an elevation of from five to ten thousand feet. Upon this broad and lofty base rise various mountain-ranges running longitudinally north and south and reaching their greatest average heights in the Rocky Mountains of Colorado and in the Sierra Nevadas

of California.   North of the Sierras lies the Cascade
range of Oregon, Washington, and British Columbia.
This chain is of volcanic structure, many of its
peaks still retaining their crater formation.   Reaching Alaska, the Cordillera breaks into a confusion of
groups and irregular ridges, and presents the highest
peaks of the continent, Mount McKinley, at the
head of Cook Inlet, attaining an altitude of 20,464
feet.   South of the United States the Cordillera
extends through Mexico and Central America, preserving the general character of the northern system—that is, a table-land of considerable height
with detached ranges and peaks; and in this region
are many active as well as extinct volcanoes.   The
highest of them are Orizaba (18,250 feet) and Popo-
catapetl (17,520 feet).

Eastward from the Cordillera stretches the great
central basin of the continent, which reaches the
Atlantic at Hudson Bay, and is bordered throughout
the United States by the Appalachian or Eastern
mountain system.   The only elevation of prominence which breaks the monotony of this expanse is made by the geographically unimportant
Ozark Mountains of Arkansas, Missouri, and Indian
Territory, rising but slightly over three thousand
feet.

The Appalachians, on the other hand, have played
a most important part in the history of the nation:
they extend from Nova Scotia in a southwesterly
direction through the eastern states to Alabama and

Georgia.   The Appalachians are not a continuous
range and exhibit many breaks and groups, but
may nevertheless be regarded as a single system.
Their highest points are found in the White Mountains of New Hampshire and the Black Mountains
of North Carolina, which reach altitudes of over
six thousand feet; the central part of the system is
seldom over three thousand feet in height, and
usually less.

Tracing this system from the north, the most
striking gap in its continuity is made by the Hudson
River, with its extension up the valley of the Mohawk to the Great Lakes and down the valley of
Lake Champlain to the St. Lawrence.   This leaves
the Adirondack Mountains of northern New York
as an isolated group, and quite cuts off the Appalachians of New England and eastern Canada from
the ridges of the south.   In New England there are
two well-marked groups of elevation, separated by
the Connecticut River—the Green and the White
mountains, which reach their greatest heights in
Vermont and New Hampshire; yet nowhere in New
England is there a sufficient elevation to offer any
very decided obstruction to migration and communication.

West and south of the Hudson Valley rises the
central division of the Appalachians, presenting
several detached groups of eminences, of which
the Catskill Mountains, in southeastern New York,
are the most conspicuous.   In Pennsylvania, New

Jersey, and the Virginias appears what may be considered the typical formation of the Appalachian system: here is found a relatively narrow plateau from seventy to two hundred miles in width, limited by the Blue Ridge on the east and the Alleghany mountains on the west. The central valley thus contained extends south practically to the termination of the range in the Gulf states. It is broken here and there by intersecting lines of hills, usually placed longitudinally, which form a great number of minor valleys, but the general character of the great central depression is nowhere lost, and it early took the significant name of "The Valley."

The arrangement of the relief of the continent breaks the lowlands into several belts. Lying between the Cordillera and the Appalachians, and occupying the greater portion of the continent, is the great central basin of North America. Extending as it does from the extreme north to the extreme south, it exhibits wide variations in climate, and hence in superficial character. In the north it is cold and barren; between latitudes fifty and sixty degrees it is covered for the most part with forests; while from fifty degrees southward stretch on the west the dry and treeless great plains and on the east the more fertile prairies.

The great plains extend from the base of the Rocky Mountains eastward, and without definite boundary merge irregularly into the prairies of the trans - Mississippi states, and drop off southward until they disappear in the richness of vegetation brought about by the increased rainfall of Mexico and Central America. They are not an unbroken expanse of level territory, but are often hilly and almost always rolling in character. The deep valleys cut by the intersecting streams further break the monotony of the region. The excessive dryness of the plains has prevented any large growth of population, but the discovery that they afford admirable grazing for horses, cattle, and sheep has brought about a development of that industry which has been of great significance in the growth of the United States and in the westward movement. The prairies, the remarkably fertile lowlands of the middle west, are seen at their best in the states of Iowa, Illinois, and Indiana, but extend well into Ohio, and were the chief attraction to early migration from the Atlantic states.

East and south of the Appalachian barrier lies a narrow strip of lowland, the Atlantic coastal plain, the seat of much of the early colonization. The water boundary of the plain is shallow, and from New Jersey to North Carolina is fringed with reefs which have forced the commercial settlements of the strip back upon the estuaries of the rivers draining the slope.

South from the Carolinas the Atlantic plain sweeps around the southern end of the Appalachian Mountains and merges into the coastal plain of the Gulf, which in turn extends south along the Texas shore into Mexico. The Gulf plain is broken and hilly in the interior, but as it approaches the coast spreads into flat and rather marshy prairies. The state of Florida offers a peculiar modification of the Atlantic plain, and appears to be a slight upheaval of the sea bottom. The most distinguishing feature of the Florida peninsula is the impenetrable wilderness in the south known as the Everglades.

West of the Rocky Mountains in the United States a wide plateau of lava formation appears in the country drained by the Columbia River and its tributaries. This area lies chiefly in Idaho, Oregon, and Washington, and was the first point occupied in the settlement of the Pacific slope from the east. South of the Columbia plateau stretches an arid territory including Nevada, parts of Utah and Arizona and southern California. Through this desert the Colorado drains to the Gulf of California, and it is the only considerable river of the area, the other streams all losing themselves in the dry soil. Between the ranges of the Pacific slope lie valleys and plains of greater or less extent, the most important being the central valley of California, the Willamette of Oregon, and the lowlands about Puget Sound, in Washington.

A striking and significant feature of North America is the chain of Great Lakes—Ontario, Erie, Huron, Michigan, and Superior—inland seas of fresh water, forming the political boundary between the United States and Canada. These lakes

drain an immense area in the interior of the continent, and their waters reach the Atlantic through
the St. Lawrence. Other great inland bodies of
water are Great Bear, Great Slave, and Athabasca
lakes in the north, which empty into the Arctic
by way of the Mackenzie River; lakes Winnipeg
and Manitoba and Lake of the Woods, which drain
into Hudson Bay, and certain desert lakes, such as
Great Salt, which have no outlets. In addition
there are thousands of smaller lakes and ponds,
particularly in the northern tier of states and in
central Canada, the depressions which they fill
having been formed for the most part by the
grinding of the great Laurentian glacier.

Generally speaking, the drainage of North America is into the Atlantic Ocean, and the larger part
goes through the outlet of the great interior basin,
the Mississippi, with its chief tributaries, the Missouri, Ohio, Arkansas, and Red rivers; or through the
St. Lawrence, with its lake supply. The northern
part of the basin is drained into the Arctic by the
Mackenzie and into Hudson Bay by various
streams, notably the Nelson River. East of the
Appalachian barrier the narrow coastal plain is
drained by a large number of streams of relatively
short flow, of which the chief are the Kennebec,
Connecticut, Hudson, Delaware, Susquehanna, Potomac, and James, all of which cut their way through
the mountain ridges to reach the sea, and all of
which played a part in determining early settlement

and provincial boundaries. Farther south the Roanoke, Yadkin, Catawba, and Savannah may be mentioned, while the southern plain is drained into the Gulf of Mexico by the Appalachicola, the Alabama, and other small streams besides the lower waters of the great Mississippi.

The true continental watershed runs irregularly through the Rocky Mountains, and west of that barrier the drainage is to the Pacific, except for a few enclosed basins. The chief western streams are the Colorado to the Gulf of California, the Columbia and the Fraser to the ocean, and the Yukon into Bering Sea.

Geologically speaking, the record of North America is simple. The oldest part of the continent is doubtless the Laurentian plateau in eastern Canada, with its extension south represented by the Adirondacks of New York, and a considerable area about the Great Lakes. From this centre the emergence seems to have been progressively westward. The Laurentian uplift was evidently in the earliest geological periods, for the structure of the rocks and the character of the deposits argue a formation deep beneath the earth's crust, with a subsequent upheaval and gradual denudation, requiring ages to effect.

The Cordilleras of the west are, on the contrary, comparatively recent and exhibit the results of late volcanic action. In Mexico active volcanoes still exist, and in Alaska they are not entirely extinct.

Many of the basins and valleys of the system are vast lava beds, forming in certain regions extensive low plateaus, as in the drainage area of the Columbia River.

A matter of prime importance for the geologist and for the student of race distribution is the record of a great glacial sheet which in very recent geological times spread over practically all of Canada and a large part of the United States. It extended south over New England and New York to the Ohio River, and westward over the prairies and a portion of the great plains. The erosive action of this glacier has been of great significance. With its retreat was discovered the great level extent of prairie land, where the drift deposit has produced most fertile soil. Along the northern frontier of the United States, and through eastern and central Canada, the ragged track of the ice sheet is marked by the thousands of lakes and watercourses which distinguish that area.

The mineral deposits of the continent are rich and varied. Of these coal is one of the most important, and, in the east at least, is so universally distributed that there is no habitable portion of the United States many miles distant from a natural supply.[1] The interior and far west are less favored, but there are, nevertheless, many spots in which coal is found. The Mexican deposits are rich but undeveloped. In 1902 the United States produced

[1] Shaler, *United States of America*, I., 428.

about one-third of the entire coal supply of the world, with an estimated value of $367,000,000.[1]

Iron is also of great importance and widely distributed, and in recent years the value of the output in the United States has exceeded that of coal. In 1902 seventy-six per cent. of the ore came from the Lake Superior district, while Alabama followed with ten per cent. of the product. Other metals of which the annual yield in the United States exceeds a value of $1,000,000 are, with their approximate values in millions, gold (80), copper (77), silver (29), lead (22), zinc (14), aluminum (2), and quicksilver ($1\frac{1}{2}$). Numerous other metals are produced in smaller quantities. Gold is found in considerable abundance in several of the western states and in Canada, Alaska, and Mexico. Silver is also a metal of wide distribution, and Mexico leads all countries of the world in its production. In the output of copper Montana is in the lead, with the Lake Superior region second. Lead is produced mainly in the West; Kansas leads in the production of zinc; and California is first in quicksilver.

Among the non-metallic mineral products are many of great significance and value, such as petroleum, natural gas, clay, borax, gypsum, salt, etc. Nearly all the mineral materials needed in the industrial life of the United States are found within its borders and in sufficient quantities. Those

[1] See for these and following figures, U. S. Geol. Survey, *Report on Mineral Resources of U. S. for 1902.*

most largely imported are tin, antimony, platinum, nickel, sulphur, and precious stones.

The climate of North America naturally varies greatly, depending on latitude, the general atmospheric circulation or direction of the prevailing winds, and the form and relief of the land areas. The influence of latitude is evident as we proceed from the tropical climate of Central America to the arctic climate of the far north. The greater part of the continent lies within the region of the anti-trades or prevailing west winds, and as a consequence the Pacific coast has an insular climate, moist and without great extremes of temperature. As the mountains lie near the coast, the winds soon lose their moisture, and the interior region east of the coastal ranges has but a slight rainfall and is largely arid or desert, presenting the wide extremes of temperature and rather light rainfall which are characteristic of a continental climate.

The rainfall gradually increases as we approach the Atlantic Ocean and the Gulf of Mexico, the great sources of supply for the eastern region. The effect of the difference in climate brought about by the prevailing winds, tempered as they are by the surface over which they have blown, is seen in the difference between the climates of similar latitudes in Labrador and southern Alaska. Proceeding from the region of the anti-trades to that of the trade winds, the conditions are reversed, and it is now the east coast which receives the rainfall. The

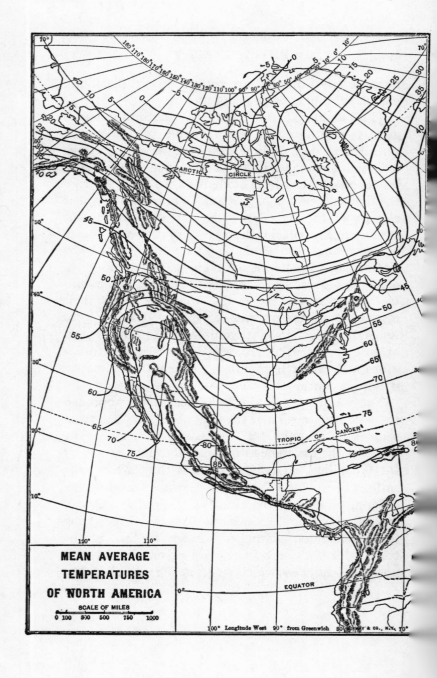

MEAN AVERAGE
TEMPERATURES
OF NORTH AMERICA

SCALE OF MILES

0 100   300   500   750   1000

100° Longitude West   90°   from Greenwich   80°   HAMMOND & CO., N.Y.   70°

difference is exhibited to a certain extent even in the United States in the increased rainfall on the southern Atlantic coast, and in the dry climate of southern California, but is more noticeable in Mexico and Central America. The contrast between the extreme temperatures of a continental climate and the more uniform conditions of a coastal climate, especially to the windward, may be readily seen by comparing the isothermal lines for January and July.

The islands belonging to North America are numerous and important. Excluding the arctic archipelago, which is composed of a number of land masses of almost continental size, the only large islands in the North Atlantic are Newfoundland, opposite the Gulf of St. Lawrence, Cape Breton, in the Gulf, and Long Island, off the mouth of the Hudson River. The tropic seas to the south abound in islands collectively called the West Indies; they include the Greater Antilles, Cuba, Haiti, Jamaica, and Porto Rico, and the Lesser Antilles, a chain of small islands stretching in a curve from Porto Rico to the South American coast, including among others Guadeloupe, Martinique, Barbadoes, and Trinidad. Southeast of Florida and north of Cuba are the Bahama Islands, on parallel 25° N. The West Indies are, geologically, a partially submerged mountain-range, and many of the smaller islands retain a volcanic character. Embraced by the West Indies and the shores of Central and South America is the Caribbean Sea.

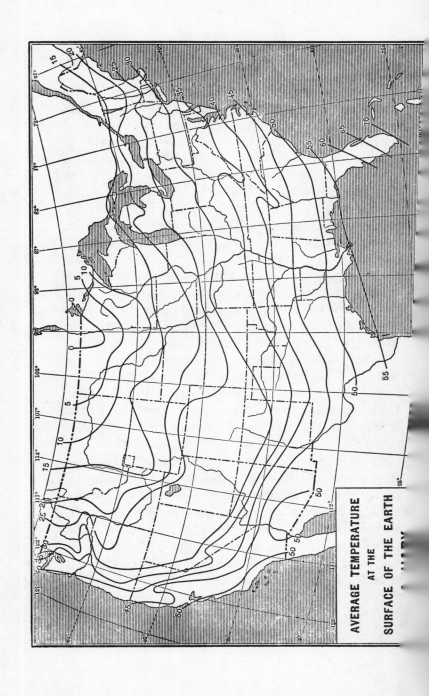

AVERAGE TEMPERATURE
AT THE
SURFACE OF THE EARTH

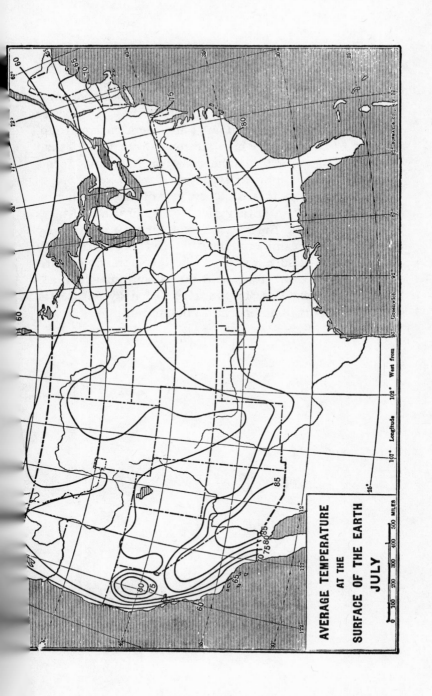

AVERAGE TEMPERATURE
AT THE
SURFACE OF THE EARTH
JULY

0 100 200 300 400 500 MILES

Off the Pacific coast the only islands of importance are Vancouver, north of Puget Sound and opposite the international boundary; and the Aleutian group, far to the north, which stretches from the Alaskan peninsula nearly to the coast of Asia and forms the southern limit of Bering Sea.

From even this rapid survey of the continental features the infinite variety of natural advantages which North America offers to man is clear. By its extensive mineral deposits, by the adaptability of its soil and climate to the development of agriculture in every form, and by its contour which admits of easy distribution, it is fitted by nature for the support of an enormous population.

CHAPTER II

WATERWAYS, PORTAGES, TRAILS, AND MOUNTAIN-PASSES

(1500–1800)

THE two most important factors in the exploration and settlement of a country are the waterways and mountain systems — the one an assistance to travel, the other an obstacle. In the sheltered bays, inlets, and rivers of the Atlantic coast of North America the early European settlements were mostly placed; but some locations were chosen well inland, up the larger rivers, and often near the head of navigation for sea-going vessels —for example, Quebec and Montreal on the St. Lawrence, where the lower shores were forbidding; and the settlements on the James and the Delaware, where fear of attack by sea determined the sites.

From these points as bases the early exploration and settlement of the country extended, and the significance of the rivers and streams at once became evident.[1] The dense forests, where the only road was the narrow Indian trail, were not passable except on foot; even pack animals could be used

---

[1] For the authorities, see chap. xviii., below.

with difficulty. The streams, however, offered a
ready means of transport and the light birch-bark
canoe, which could be shouldered over the necessary
portages, made it possible for the early voyageurs to
penetrate far into the heart of the continent, carrying their merchandise for barter and returning with
their bales of furs. River travel on east and west
lines involved crossings from one stream to another;
hence a point of great interest to the pioneer was
the portage.

From the Atlantic seaboard the St. Lawrence
and the Great Lakes offered the readiest access to
the interior of the continent, and as a natural consequence we find the French, the settlers of the
St. Lawrence basin, the first explorers of a large
part of the interior of North America; and this, too,
before the English farther south had even passed
the Alleghanies. By portages from Lake Superior to
Rainy Lake and thence to Lake of the Woods, the
French gained the northward-flowing streams and
penetrated to Hudson Bay and far into the Canadian
northwest. Their successors, the English and Scotch
of the fur companies, were the first to reach the
Pacific coast from the interior. It is interesting,
too, that the first portage to the Mississippi Valley
discovered by explorers was one of those lying
farthest west—that from the Fox River to the
Wisconsin.

The place and convenience of these portages were
well known to the Indian, and the European as a

rule merely followed the trail of the savage. Their importance in the early occupation of the country is attested by the fact that forts were immediately established on most of the main portages; and in the French and Indian wars such places as Crown Point, Schenectady, and Presque Isle indicated lines of attack and defence. Since these routes followed the lowest and easiest ways over the watersheds between the river valleys, wagon-roads and railways were eventually built along the same lines, which thus exerted a marked influence both on the early movements of population and the more recent developments of commercial centres.

In Canada one of the most important portages was that from the upper Ottawa to Lake Nipissing, from which the French River was followed to Georgian Bay and Lake Huron. The route left the Ottawa by way of the Mattawa River, up which it passed to Trout Lake; thence across the low divide by an easy carry to Rivière de la Vase, a small stream emptying into Lake Nipissing, about five miles south of North Bay. This is nearly the line of the Canadian Pacific Railway.[1] In the early days of the occupation this was the main route to the West, more used than a second passage from Lake Ontario by the river Trent across to Lake Simcoe and thence to Lake Huron.

From the upper end of Lake Superior two well-known portages led over the divide to the waters

[1] Geol. Survey, Canada, *Annual Report*, 1897, X., H. 12.

of the Northwest: the Grand Portage, from the
bay of that name, or from Pigeon River, which
empties into it, across to Rainy Lake and Lake of
the Woods; the other from Thunder Bay up the
Kaministiquia and Dog River, and across by Lac
des Mille Lacs and Sturgeon Lake and River to
Rainy Lake.   The latter was the route commonly
followed by the early fur-traders; and the Northwest Company later established one of its principal
stations at Fort William on Thunder Bay.   This
route was of great assistance in the construction of
the Canadian Pacific Railway, which also runs from
Fort William up the Kaministiquia and crosses the
divide not far from the old portage trail.

From the Great Lakes to the Mississippi basin
there was a choice of paths.   In the Northwest the
French often crossed from the head of Lake Superior
to the upper Mississippi by way of the St. Louis
River.   The most important portage, however, was
probably that which led from the Fox to the
Wisconsin River, first used in 1673 by Joliet and
Marquette,[1] and later the site of Fort Winnebago.
At the southern end of Lake Michigan an important
trail led from the Chicago to the Des Plaines and
so to the Illinois, on the same line as the present
Chicago Drainage Canal; the portage was from four
to nine miles in length according to the season.
Other carrying-places of that region were from the
Calumet to the Des Plaines, and from the St.

---

[1] *Jesuit Relations* (Thwaites' ed.), LIX., 105, 107.

Joseph to the Kankakee; but that from the St. Joseph to the Wabash was the principal channel of supplies for the early settlers at Vincennes.

On account of the hostility of the Iroquois Indians, the portages from Lake Erie were not much used until the eighteenth century, but later became of great importance. On the west there was one well-known and much-frequented portage from the Maumee to the Wabash which varied from eight to twenty miles in length. Its eastern end is marked by the present town of Fort Wayne. Two portages led from the Maumee to Loramie Creek, a branch of the Great Miami. General Wayne built Fort Loramie near the southern end of these portages in 1794. Other carries were from the Sandusky to the Scioto; from the Cuyahoga, near the present city of Akron, Ohio, to the Tuscarawas and the Muskingum, and from the neighborhood of Ravenna to the Mahoning; from Lake Erie at Presque Isle (the present site of Erie) to the French Creek and the Alleghany; and from Lake Erie to Chautauqua Lake and thence to the Alleghany River.[1] The carry around Niagara Falls was, of course, much used, though there was another route from Lake Ontario by portage to Grand River and thence to Lake Erie.

One of the most important portages in the early history of the colonies was the "Oneida," which varied with the stage of the water from four to

[1] Young, *Hist. of Chautauqua County*, 37–44.

eight miles in length. It led from the Mohawk
Valley to Wood Creek, a tributary of the Oswego,
and so to Lake Ontario. This was the strategic
point on the route from New York and the Hudson
to the Great Lakes. In 1732 Fort William was
erected at the Mohawk terminus, where is now the
city of Rome, and in 1758 this was replaced by the
famous Fort Stanwix. Forts were also established
near the other end of the portage.[1]

Another series of much-frequented carrying-
places were on the "Grand Pass" leading from the
valley of the Hudson into Canada, the line of
numerous French invasions from the north and of
Burgoyne's expedition in 1777. The main portage
of this route, that from the Hudson to Lake George,
was about fifteen miles long and was guarded by
Fort Edward on the Hudson and by Fort William
Henry at the southern end of Lake George. Another important portage on this route was from
Lake George to Lake Champlain, guarded by Fort
Ticonderoga. Still another route between the Hudson and Lake Champlain was from Fort Edward,
northeast over a portage of about eleven miles
to Wood Creek and down that stream to the lake.
Fort Ann was built on Wood Creek to protect this
route.

Farther east a number of portages led from the
rivers of New England to the St. Lawrence basin—

[1] Sylvester, *Northern New York and the Adirondack Wilderness*, 280.

for example, the important Indian trail from the Connecticut to the St. Francis; that from the Kennebec and Dead River to the Chaudière, crossed by Arnold in 1775;[1] and several from the headwaters of the St. John northward.

From the Atlantic coast to the Ohio Valley the main portages were from the Susquehanna to the Alleghany near Kittanning; from the Juniata to the Alleghany, the present route of the Pennsylvania Railroad; and from the Potomac to the Monongahela, *via* Wills Creek, the line of Braddock's march. Farther south the portage probably most used was from the headwaters of the James to the Greenbrier branch of the Kanawha. These southerly routes, though important Indian trails, were never much used by the whites, because the streams were not favorable to navigation by large boats; moreover, the trails were long and rough, and lay to one side of the main lines of travel. The more northern routes to the upper Ohio were also too long and difficult to be of much value for the transport of goods in colonial times.

To the settler, with his household goods and farming implements, falls and rapids made the Appalachian streams practically impassable for his transportation, and wagon-roads were indispensable for his movements on land. Such roads are ordinarily not built until demanded by military opera-

[1] Smith, "Arnold's Battle with the Wilderness," in *Century Magazine*, LXV., 529.

tions or extensive movements of population. Hence
the spread of population on the Atlantic seaboard
proceeded rapidly enough up-stream to the heads
of navigation, but from those points inland progress was much slower and was entirely checked by
the mountain-ranges until roads were constructed
across them.

Of all the routes by which the Appalachian
barrier could be crossed, the most favorable in the
north was by way of the Hudson and Mohawk
valleys to the lakes; but it was closed to the early
settlers by the Iroquois, though subsequently of
immense importance. A second route was from
the headwaters of the Mohawk to the upper Alleghany. A third route was through southern Pennsylvania to the Monongahela and so to the Ohio
River. The fourth well-travelled route was by the
broad Appalachian Valley to the southwest and out
through Cumberland Gap or the valley of the Tennessee to the more open country beyond. It would
also have been possible to go around the southern
end of the Appalachian chain, but this way was
closed until comparatively modern times by the
Cherokee Indians. In the first settlement of the
Ohio Valley the routes by Cumberland Gap and
the Tennessee were the most important; but with
the later improvement of the more direct roads
through Pennsylvania these roundabout paths fell
into disuse.

The discovery of these ways was not a matter of

chance. In every case they followed more or less closely the line of an Indian trail.[1] In crossing the divides and mountain-ranges the trails followed the gentlest slopes and traversed the lowest gaps; but elsewhere they kept to the higher levels, following the ridges and uplands between the valleys in order to avoid swamps and streams. As the Indians travelled in single file their trails were merely narrow runways through the forest, often worn to a depth of a foot or more and winding about to avoid obstacles. In addition to the trails of the Indian there were also the tracks of the buffalo, though the two often followed the same path, especially across the mountain passes.

The Indians at times travelled great distances, and many of their trails connected widely separated regions. Some of the more extensive of these primitive lines of communication became widely known under special names. In New England important trails led from different points of the coast up to and beyond the Connecticut Valley, one of the best-known being the Old Connecticut Path from Boston, by way of Grafton, Oxford, and Springfield, to Albany.

The most famous Indian thoroughfare in New York was the great Iroquois war-trail from the Hudson up the Mohawk Valley and westward along the water-shed to the Niagara River. It was the great highway connecting the different tribes

[1] Hulbert, *Indian Thoroughfares.*

of the Iroquois with one another and with the regions to the east and west.

In Pennsylvania there was an important trading trail running from Philadelphia up the Susquehanna and Juniata, across the Alleghany Mountains by Kittanning Gorge and down to the Alleghany River. A branch of this trail ran farther south by way of Raystown (Bedford) to the junction of the Alleghany and Monongahela. To this point also ran a trail from the Potomac, sometimes called Nemacolin's Path, from the name of a Delaware chief.

One of the most noted of the early trails was the Great Indian War-path of Virginia, up the Shenandoah Valley, across the headwaters of the New River to the upper Holston, and on down to the Cherokee territory of east Tennessee and Georgia. It was joined in Tennessee by the Warrior's Path from Ohio, sometimes called the Scioto Trail, which started at Sandusky on Lake Erie, followed up the Sandusky River, and down the Scioto to its mouth. Across the Ohio it led south through Kentucky and Cumberland Gap to its junction with the Virginia trail in eastern Tennessee. This was the great war-path from the north, the line of the principal invasions from both north and south, and was used by the whites as well as by the Indians. A branch of the Scioto Trail also followed up the Kanawha and across the mountains to the headwaters of the James.

Another well-known route from north to south was the Miami Trail. North of the Ohio it had several branches in the Little and Great Miami valleys, but they all converged on the Ohio River near the mouth of the Licking. After crossing the Ohio the trail ran south to the water-shed between the Green and the Cumberland rivers, where it forked, one branch continuing straight on to the Cherokee country, while the other joined the Scioto Trail on its way through Cumberland Gap.

An important effect of the topography of America on its history is seen in the development of the important roads which were later constructed along the line of the old Indian routes. Of these Braddock's Road followed Nemacolin's Path; and the Cumberland Road, built early in the nineteenth century, took the same line over the divide. The road to Pittsburg, finished by General Forbes in 1758,[1] followed the old trading trail through Carlisle, Shippensburg, and Bedford, and soon became the main thoroughfare to its objective point, though Braddock's Road was much used by those coming from Virginia.

Another important route was discovered when progress westward from Virginia was stopped by the Alleghany range and the Cumberland escarpment; and the early pioneers turned south along the great valley into western Virginia and eastern Tennessee, following the old war-path to the Cherokee district. Having thus rounded the mountains, the

[1] Hulbert, *Old Glade Road.*

route followed the Ohio trail through Cumberland Gap. This way was first opened by Daniel Boone, and was variously known as "Boone's Trail," the "Kentucky Road," and the "Wilderness Road." [1] Beginning at the settlements on the upper Holston, it passed westward by openings in the valley ranges across Cumberland Gap to the Cumberland River, where it left the old Indian trail and followed a buffalo trace through Boone's Gap to Fort Boonesborough on the Kentucky River, and thence on to Lexington. This road, which until 1796 was only a pack-trail, opened up central Kentucky and Tennessee to the Virginia and Carolina settlers; and even those from Pennsylvania sometimes preferred this route. As the northern roads to the Ohio improved, however, they attracted most of the travellers, who, after striking the Ohio, descended that river by boat, and followed up its branches to their various destinations.

Access had thus been gained to the very heart of the Mississippi Valley, and after the Revolution immigration poured down the river and up its tributaries in a never-ending stream. Then the waterways became of less importance, since the generally level character of the country permitted the easy construction of wagon-roads. The influence of the streams was still potent, nevertheless, and the advancing wave of population presented a ragged front due to the more rapid progress along their courses.

[1] Speed, *Wilderness Road;* Hulbert, *Boone's Wilderness Road.*

As the arid regions of the great plains were gained, the advance was checked and the country to the rear was quickly filled.

The streams flowing eastward from the Rockies, with the exception of the Missouri, were only navigable during a portion of the year, and as a consequence were unsuitable as lines of travel. The Missouri as the one copious river was the natural highway, therefore, and was ascended by Lewis and Clark in 1804 in their memorable journey to the Pacific.[1] Proceeding to the headwaters by boat, they crossed the Bitter Root Mountains by the northern Nez Percé or Lou Lou Trail, one of the most difficult in the country and one which has seldom been followed since. Descending on the west to the Clearwater, they continued by boat down the Snake and Columbia to the sea. Even before Lewis and Clark's expedition, hunters and trappers had penetrated to the Rocky Mountains, but the great distances to be travelled and the forbidding character of the country checked for a considerable time the westward movement of settlers.

At the opening of the last century St. Louis was the starting - point and base of supplies for the Western traders. Later the centre moved west to Franklin, on the Missouri, then to Independence, and finally to Kansas City, where the river turned north.[2]

[1] Coues, *Hist. of the Lewis and Clark Expedition.*
[2] Gregg, *Commerce of the Prairies*, I., 32; Inman, *Old Santa Fé Trail*, 145.

To this point the western trails converged, with the exception of one or two which passed along the more southern tributaries of the Mississippi.

As the Spaniards or Mexicans already had settlements in New Mexico and California, endeavors were soon made to establish trade with those points, and the Santa Fé Trail was the first important road of the West.[1] This road, about eight hundred miles long, passed westward from Independence to the Arkansas, up that stream to Bent's Fort, thence southwest up Timpas Creek and across the Raton Pass to Las Vegas and San Miguel. From this point it pushed westward through Apache Cañon to the Santa Fé Valley. This trail was not favorable for wagons, and as their use increased, a more southerly route was adopted, which left the Arkansas, passed southwest to the Cimarron, and up that stream, meeting the old trail at Las Vegas.

From New Mexico two routes were discovered to the Pacific coast. One ran from the Rio Grande over the divide to the headwaters of the Gila River and down to the Colorado and southern California. As the route along the upper Gila was difficult for wagons, a way was found around the mountains farther south, near the present line of the Southern Pacific Railroad.[2] The other trail led from Santa Fé northwest up the Chama River and

---

[1] Chittenden, *American Fur Trade of the Far West;* Inman, *Old Santa Fé Trail.*

[2] Emory, in *Ex. Docs.*, 30 Cong., 1 Sess., No. 41.

down the Dolores Valley, crossing the Grand River near the present site of Moab, Utah. It then led over to the Sevier, southwest up that stream, and down the Virgin. Instead of continuing to the Colorado, the trail turned west towards California, crossing the Mojave Desert and Cajon Pass, and terminated at San Bernardino and Los Angeles. This route was known as the Spanish Trail and was much used for many years.[1] Frémont, on his return from California in 1844, followed this trail as far as Utah.

To the north the early settlers reached the Pacific slope over what came to be widely known as the Oregon Trail. This was about two thousand miles in length. It followed the Platte, its north fork, and the Sweetwater to South Pass; thence across the Green River, up Black River and Muddy Creek, and over the divide into Bear River Valley, which it left to cross to Fort Hall on the Snake. Following the Snake River to a point below Salmon Falls, the trail cut across the plains to Fort Boisé, and thence down the Snake again to Burnt River. Ascending Burnt River Cañon it crossed to the upper Powder, thence over the divide of the Blue Mountains, and down the Umatilla to the Columbia. Movement along the Oregon Trail began about 1832, and by 1845 there were eight thousand Americans in the valley of the Columbia.[2]

A southward movement had begun almost im-

---

[1] Bancroft, *Hist. of California*, III., 386.
[2] Monette, *Hist. of the Mississippi Valley*, II., 569.

mediately from the Columbia River into the Sacramento Valley of California, and a demand arose for a more direct route to that country. After several unsuccessful and somewhat disastrous attempts[1] to find a suitable pass over the Sierras, Truckee Pass was discovered in 1844,[2] and the California Trail became definitely established. This route left the Oregon Trail at Bear River, crossed northern Nevada by way of the Humboldt River to Truckee River, ascended that stream, crossed the Truckee Pass, and descended the Bear River to the Sacramento. This was the route followed in after years by the Central Pacific Railroad.

Such are the main lines by which native migration and the later exploration and settlement by the whites have proceeded. Their significance for the history and development of the country is obvious. Other factors have naturally had their influence; but in determining the direction of the flow as well as the location of the chief centres of population geographical conditions have been paramount. With the advance of civilization and the acquisition of new modes of transportation, geographical exigencies become less rigorous, but they still remain the leading factor in determining the location and growth of centres of population.

[1] Bancroft, *Hist. of California*, IV., 269–271, 394, 438.
[2] *Ibid.*, 446.

CHAPTER III

TIMBER AND AGRICULTURAL PRODUCTS OF NORTH AMERICA

(1500-1900)

NEXT to purely geographical considerations the character and distribution of the vegetable products have probably played the most important part in determining the direction and permanence of the settlement of the different parts of North America. From one point of view the distribution of plant life is simply the working out of variation in soil and climate; but to the native as well as to the immigrant the product of the soil and not the cause of that product demands first attention. Hence the presence or absence of forests and the character of the available vegetable food supply have not only modified the cultures of the Indian groups, but have regulated and determined the flow of civilized population.

The forest belt of the continent extends far to the north, including nearly the whole of Labrador, everything south of a line drawn from the middle of the western shore of Hudson Bay to the mouth of the Mackenzie River, and all of Alaska except the extreme northwest. In the northern belt the trees are the same or similar across the continent, and but few species appear, the most typical being the poplars and the black and white spruces, which near their northern limit are stunted and of no economic importance, but farther south yield valuable timber.

On the east the forest originally formed an unbroken sheet along the entire Atlantic coast as far south as central Florida, and along the Gulf shore into Texas, the general western boundary of the forest reaching or even crossing the Mississippi. The Pacific belt ceases to connect with the Atlantic at about the sixtieth parallel, near the eastern slopes of the Rocky Mountains; there the prairies interfere and form along the western edge of the Atlantic forest a broad area which is but slightly wooded.

A short distance south of the forty-ninth parallel the wooded region of the Pacific forks, the coast division being densely covered with very valuable timber, while the Rocky Mountains in many parts are also well supplied with trees. Between these two Pacific groups, and even more in the wide extent of country between the Rocky Mountains and the western edge of the prairies, trees are practically wanting. The main factor in determining this distribution is the rainfall; in dry regions trees are few or absent, although in limited regions they may be raised by water conducted from a river or other source of supply through artificial channels and distributed over the land as required.

The trees on the two sides of the continent are
sharply differentiated. While in the northeast the
conifers, or soft woods, form the prevailing element,
there is, nevertheless, a considerable mixture of
hardwoods with deciduous, broad leaves; and farther
south the latter constitute almost the entire forest,
except along the coastal plain. On the Pacific the
reverse is true, the conifers reaching a size and
luxuriance unequalled elsewhere, while the hardwoods are comparatively few.

The most important species in the east has been
the white pine, formerly very abundant in eastern
Canada and south as far as Massachusetts, but extending in less quantity south of that limit. For
many years the main supply has been drawn from
its western range in northern Michigan, Wisconsin,
and Minnesota. So freely has it been cut that
even in that region it is becoming extinct for
practical purposes. The original quantity is estimated to have been seven hundred billion feet,[1]
and the average cut at present is about two billion
feet annually.

In the northeast are many other species of conifers, such as various kinds of pine, the white cedar,
hemlock, fir, larch, and the spruces already mentioned. The most important hardwoods are the sugar
and red maples, the beech, various birches (especially the canoe birch), the white elm, and the

[1] *The White Pine* (U. S. Dept. Agric., Div. of Forestry,
Bulletin 22), p. 19.

white ash. In the central states the conifers lose their importance and hardwoods take the chief place. The most notable trees of this class are the oaks (represented by about twenty-five species), several kinds of hickory, the chestnut, the black walnut (once very valuable, but now exhausted), the basswood, the magnolias, the tupelo, the tulip-tree, and the cotton-wood. Although a conifer, the hemlock is at its best in the mountains of North Carolina.

Besides the lumber actually used, an enormous quantity has inevitably been destroyed in clearing the land, and forest fires have also wrought great damage. As a result, lumbering has ceased to be an important industry over most of this region, though much is still done in places, the chief hard-wood centres being at present Tennessee and Kentucky.

On the coasts of the southern states, not only on the Atlantic but along the Gulf of Mexico as far as Texas, and extending up the Mississippi into Missouri, are several valuable pines, especially the long-leaf, the short-leaf, and the loblolly. From the first of these and a fourth species, the slash pine, the turpentine of commerce is derived.

Southern Florida differs much from the rest of the country, its plants having many features in common with those of the West Indies. A considerable number of the Antillean trees extend to the continent, but are not as a rule well developed, except the mahogany and the royal palm; while the sea-shores have a tropical border of mangroves.

The western trees are nearly all soft woods and often attain gigantic dimensions. The variety is not great, but with some notable exceptions each kind has a wide distribution. To the north spruces, poplars, and the canoe birch prevail as on the opposite side of the continent; but in the important forest region from southern British Columbia into California grow trees peculiar to the district. The most important of these, the red or Douglas fir, reaches its best development around Puget Sound and for some distance north and south of that region. It grows from two to three hundred feet in height, and is associated with other fine trees, notably the tide-land spruce, the hemlock, and the red cedar. To the east of the Cascade range, though still present, these species become less important than the yellow pine. In southern Oregon the Port Orford cedar becomes common, and is followed at the Californian border by the redwood. This last covers a rather narrow belt along the coast, but has a very dense growth, and often attains a height of two hundred and fifty or three hundred feet.

The western slopes of the Sierra Nevada also bear a very heavy forest growth, widest in northern California, and characterized by the sugar pine, the red fir, yellow pine, two true firs, and the white cedar. Most famous of all is the Big Tree (*Sequoia gigantea*), which, though neither the tallest nor the broadest, is conceded the distinction of being the largest in the world, rising to a height of from two hundred and seventy-five feet to nearly four hundred feet, with a diameter of twenty to thirty-five feet, and attaining a great age. All these are conifers. Hardwoods are, however, not entirely lacking, the most valuable in the coast region being the cotton-wood and the large-leaved maple.

In the interior the forest is less continuous. The Columbia basin contains a fair supply of timber, especially the western larch, and the eastern slopes of the Sierra Nevada bear valuable pines. In the Rocky Mountains of Colorado, at elevations of from eight to ten thousand feet, a spruce (*Picea Engelmanni*) grows luxuriantly, and yellow pine, red fir, and white fir are plentiful at lower altitudes. A similar vegetation follows the high mountains as far as western Texas, where the pines again become important.

Along the northern boundary of Mexico a fusion takes place between the floras of the adjacent portions of the Atlantic and Pacific belts. The trees are comparatively small, the mesquite extending over a very wide area, while east of the Colorado the giant cactus is one of the most striking of the plants.

This vast extent of forest has had a vital bearing upon the settlement and further development of the country. To the pioneer it was at once a blessing and a curse, supplying abundance of building material and fuel at his very door, while, on the other hand, before the land could be cultivated, arduous labor was entailed in the removal of the trees and the tearing of their roots from the ground. During the Indian wars, too, they formed an effectual screen for the advancing enemy.

From the forest various products useful as food were obtained, though these have naturally had a diminishing importance. Many kinds of shell fruits, such as chestnuts, beech, hazel, hickory, pecan, walnuts and butternuts, were used in this way, besides wild cherries and plums. The sap of the maple also yielded excellent sugar to the aborigines as well as to the pioneers. Most of the trees important for food purposes are of foreign origin, the great diversity of soil and climate making it possible to grow plants of nearly all countries not strictly tropical. Skilful cultivation and care in the selection of suitable varieties have led to the extension of many species of fruits over a wide area, so that fruit of the same kind is placed upon the market over a long period of time, the first coming from the most southern range and then from points successively farther north.

The fruit of most general and varied use is the apple, a native of Europe and Asia, but introduced into America by the early settlers. It has a great number of cultivated varieties, of which several are of importance in this country. It grows well in

Canada, in many of the northern states, and in California, in which state the fruit industry reaches its greatest development, extremely large quantities being annually shipped to the east, both in a fresh condition and preserved. Also of high economic importance are the pear, the cherries, and plums, with a northern preference, the peach, almond, quince, prune, olive, fig, and apricot, which require a warmer climate. The orange and the lemon are very largely grown in southern California and to a less extent in Florida, where also some West Indian products, such as the pineapple, are coming into cultivation.

From the economic stand-point the cereals are of supreme interest, as they furnish a very high percentage of the world's food supply. These include wheat, maize, or Indian-corn, rice, oats, rye, barley, and buckwheat, which have a variable comparative importance in different countries.

In the United States corn is the greatest of all crops, the yield for 1902[1] the greatest yet recorded, being over two billion five hundred million bushels, grown on the vast area of ninety-four million acres.[2] The plant is in all probability a native of Central America, and was generally in use among the Indians on the arrival of the whites, who found it in cultivation, and saw it employed for a vari-

---

[1] The year 1902 has, for purposes of convenience, been chosen for such comparisons as are made in the following pages.

[2] U. S. Dept. Agric., *Year-Book*, 1902, pp. 760 ff.

ety of purposes, from Peru to the St. Lawrence.
While it is grown to some extent all over the United
States, it prefers a warm climate with moderate
elevation. In 1902 Illinois produced over three
hundred and seventy-two million bushels, Iowa,
with nearly three hundred million, coming next.
Missouri and Nebraska also produced over two
hundred and fifty million, but Kansas alone of all
the other states exceeds two hundred million.
Only two others, Indiana and Ohio, produced one
hundred million, and of the remainder, Kentucky
is the only one which approaches that figure. In
contrast, the New England states together produced
only something over five million bushels.

These figures are only partially due to average
yield per acre, the New England states standing
uniformly high in this regard, though proportions
vary widely from year to year. Illinois supplied
the greatest acreage of corn cultivation—viz., over
nine million six hundred thousand. Iowa devoted
nine million three hundred thousand; Nebraska,
seven million eight hundred thousand acres to corn
alone; Kansas, seven million four hundred and fifty
thousand; Missouri, six million seven hundred and
seventy-five thousand; and Texas, five million five
hundred thousand acres. Extreme contrast is supplied by Wyoming with two thousand four hundred
acres; Montana, three thousand seven hundred;
Idaho, five thousand; and Arizona seven thousand
five hundred. Over three-fourths of the amount

shipped outside the county where it is grown came
from the five states of Illinois, Nebraska, Kansas,
Missouri, and Indiana.

Wheat is in some respects of still greater importance, but in the United States has only about
one-half the acreage of corn. Introduced by the
earliest immigrants, it was at first cultivated
throughout the East, and was carried forward with
the advance of colonization. It is distinctly a
northern crop, nowhere flourishing south of the
glaciated belt, its centre of distribution lying in the
West. In 1902 the total crop in the United States
was over six hundred and seventy million bushels,
and in North America seven hundred and eighty
million, a decrease of sixty-six million from the
figures for 1901.[1] Of this Minnesota supplied the
largest share, over ten per cent. of the whole; North
Dakota nearly sixty-three million, Missouri over
fifty-six million, Manitoba nearly fifty-five million,
and Nebraska fifty-three million bushels. Kansas
and South Dakota yielded each between forty
and fifty million Ohio, Indiana, and Illinois between thirty and forty million bushels. The best
yield per acre, twenty-nine and one-tenth bushels,
was in Washington, with something over a million
acres in cultivation, and other high averages are
made by states with a comparatively small total output. In the year chosen for comparison the continent produced almost exactly one-quarter of the

U. S. Dept. Agric., *Year-Book*, 1902, p. 268.

total supply of the world, and in the preceding year a yet higher percentage, whereas it furnished almost sixty per cent. of the world's export.

Oats also are of high importance, the crop for 1902 reaching nearly one billion bushels, grown on twenty-eight million acres, and valued at over $300,000,000. Illinois and Iowa, the former with one hundred and fifty-three million bushels, the latter with one hundred and twenty-five million bushels, produced in each case by about four million acres, are far in the lead in both product and acreage. It also is notably a northern crop, a fact attested by the Ontario yield of one hundred and ten million bushels.

Barley is less important both actually and relatively, the crop in 1902 being one hundred and thirty-five million bushels. The centres of distribution are more widely scattered, California with nearly thirty million bushels, Minnesota with twenty-six million, Wisconsin and North Dakota with sixteen million each, and Iowa with thirteen million bushels, being responsible for the great bulk of barley production.

Rye is of still less consequence, particularly in comparison with Europe, where in many parts it is the principal cereal. The 1902 output was thirty-three million bushels, most of which came from Wisconsin, Nebraska, Michigan, and Minnesota. Buckwheat, while not strictly a cereal, may be mentioned here, with an output of fourteen million five hundred thousand bushels, of which over two-thirds is raised in New York and Pennsylvania.

Rice is typically a plant of warm countries and requires a very wet soil for its growth. Before the coming of the whites the Indians obtained a considerable proportion of their food from the wild rice which grew not only in such states as Virginia, but in the Northeast and as far west as Minnesota. The cultivated species is probably a native of Hindustan, and in this country it has been grown only in the southern states. At first the bulk of the yield was produced by the Carolinas and by Georgia, Louisiana beginning to be important about forty years ago. The former states now grow a much smaller quantity, while the last-named, with Texas, form the centre of the industry. Even now the yield, about one hundred and fifty million pounds annually, is only half of the quantity consumed in the country.

The sugar-cane is a tropical plant, which in the United States is produced almost entirely in the extreme South, Louisiana furnishing nearly the entire output for the country. This is but a fraction of the amount consumed, the balance being imported from the Hawaiian Islands, West and East Indies, and South America.

Two other plants, exclusive of the maple, also contribute to the sugar supply. One is the beet, very extensively grown for this purpose in Europe. It was first employed in this country for sugar-making in 1830, but was of little consequence for a long time, the annual output of beet-sugar not reaching one thousand tons until 1888. It rose to forty thousand tons within ten years. It requires a very different climate from the cane, its ideal area being a belt about two hundred miles wide stretching from New York to the Dakotas, then passing to the Mexican border, and north and west to include the whole of California and about half of Oregon and Washington.[1] While insignificant as yet beside the European supply, the increase is very rapid, the sugar produced in 1902[2] being six times the quantity only four years before.

Of hay, sixty million tons was the total for 1902. New York raises over one-tenth of the whole from five million acres, and Iowa, Missouri, Illinois, Ohio, Pennsylvania, Wisconsin, Kansas, and Michigan follow in the order named. Besides this a vast quantity of grass is of course consumed as pasturage, alike in the east and on the great ranches in the west and southwest.

The greatest of all crops in the south is cotton. There is much doubt as to whether some variety of it was not known to the natives of Peru and Mexico before the coming of Europeans, but its culture in the United States almost certainly dates from the year of the settlement of Jamestown. It

[1] Wiley, *The Sugar Beet* (U. S. Dept. Agric., *Farmers' Bulletin*, 1899, 52).
[2] U. S. Dept. Agric., *Year-Book*, 1902, p. 825.

spread rapidly through the south, the centre of production keeping steadily ahead of that of population. Still, in 1790, the total production was less than nine thousand bales.[1] It reached two hundred and ten thousand bales in the early part of the last century. Subject to annual variations, this had risen by the beginning of the civil war to nearly five million bales. During the years of conflict the quantity fell almost to zero, and the industry did not immediately recover, though the product is now twice as large as at any time before the war. The United States produces about three-fourths of the world's supply and exports about two-thirds of its crop. At times the proportion of export has been much higher, but the growth of the manufacturing industry has more than kept pace with the increase in the crop, great though that has been. Texas furnishes the largest amount for any one state, about one-fourth of the whole. The total yield of 1902 was valued at $511,000,000 for the cotton alone. The cotton-seed industry has so far advanced that in 1902 one hundred and nineteen million gallons of oil were produced, and of oil cake over a million tons.[2]

The other characteristic southern crop is tobacco, indigenous and found in general use by the early discoverers. Kentucky produced in 1902 about

[1] U. S. Dept. Agric., Official Exper. Stations, *The Cotton-Plant Bulletin* (1896), 33.
[2] U. S. Dept. Agric., *Year-Book*, 1902, p. 816.

two hundred and fifty-eight million pounds, North Carolina one hundred and forty-two million, and Virginia one hundred and thirty-six million pounds. Wisconsin, Ohio, and Tennessee come next in order of importance, while South Carolina, Pennsylvania, Connecticut, and Maryland all yield crops of value.[1]

Vegetables and small fruits are of course grown in enormous variety wherever agriculture is practised. Of these, potatoes are the most important, and amount to over two hundred and eighty million bushels annually. Of the states Wisconsin, New York, Pennsylvania, Michigan, Illinois, Iowa, Ohio, Minnesota, Missouri, Nebraska, Kansas, and Maine, all reach the ten-million-bushel mark in potato production.

Two impressions are left by this study of American products: one is the immense variety of plant growth due to the wide variations in climate and character of the continent; and the other is that the majority of the plants of great economic value are of foreign origin. In any case the fertility and adaptability of the soil must be regarded as among the chief contributing causes to the stupendous growth of the American nation.

[1] U. S. Dept. Agric., *Year-Book*, 1902, p. 819.

CHAPTER IV

ANIMAL LIFE OF NORTH AMERICA
(1500–1900)

ANY general discussion of the continent in its relation to history must include a description of its fauna so far as it has affected the settlement of the country. From the stand-point of human interest the vertebrates are immeasurably more significant than any other forms of animal life; but it will be necessary to select those vertebrates which are indigenous, neglecting such as have been introduced by Europeans, such as the domesticated animals and the domestic animals run wild, as broncos, mustangs, and cattle of the western plains. The insects might also be considered of importance to man because of their destructive relations to agriculture and forestry.

Almost any given animal inhabits a more or less restricted geographic area, known as its "range," the limits of which are determined by climatic conditions (temperature and moisture) or by the interrelation of land areas, since intervening bodies of water serve as barriers to the dispersal of the species. Of these two factors temperature is vastly

54

more potent than moisture, and naturalists have
been able to demonstrate a remarkably close corre-
lation of life zones to isothermal lines.[1]

It is important to recall the close geographic
proximity of Alaska to the northeastern part of the
great continents of Europe and Asia, called by
geographers Eurasia. Indeed, the two continents
were probably united in the Tertiary period, as
appears from the general continuity of the circumpolar frozen region, and the similarity in physical
features and climate of the northern halves of both
land masses. To facilitate the comparative study
of animal life, naturalists have divided the earth's
surface into so-called zoögeographic areas. Of the
various schemes proposed the most logical and most
convenient for our purposes recognizes the close
similarity of the Eurasian and North American
faunas.[2] It includes in an arctic realm the entire
land area north of the annual isotherm of 32° F.;
the area between the isotherms of 32° F. and 70° F.
in the north temperate realm. The portions of
these realms falling within North America are
designated respectively as the North American
arctic region and the North American temperate
region. The latter comprises almost the entire

[1] Merriam, "The Geographic Distribution of Life in North
America" (Biological Society, *Proceedings*, VII.); "Laws of
Temperature Control of the Geographic Distribution of Terrestrial Animals and Plants" (National Geog. Soc., *Magazine*, VI.)
[2] Allen, *Geographical Distribution of North American Animals*,
206.

MAIN ZOÖGEOGRAPHIC AREAS
OF NORTH AMERICA

SCALE OF MILES
0 100   300   500   750   1000

continent, and is subdivided into cold temperate and warm temperate sub - regions, the line of division being the isotherm of 43° F., or, roughly speaking, the boundary-line between Canada and the United States. South of the North American temperate region is the American tropical realm, including Central America, the West Indies, and a part of Mexico, Florida, and Lower California.

Proceeding to a survey of the fauna of North America, and taking first the American arctic region, the area beyond the tree limit, we find that it has no specific fauna. Its animal inhabitants are all circumpolar in distribution, and occur also in arctic Eurasia. The most notable arctic animals are the polar bear, arctic fox, arctic hare, the musk-ox (now extinct in the Old World), the white lemming, barren-ground caribou, the walrus, and, among birds, the willow ptarmigan. The seals are abundant, but certain species found in the eastern (Barren Ground) and western (Alaskan) groups are not identical.

Passing to the north temperate realm we find a sharp distinction from the fauna of the arctic region.[1] The total number of genera of land mammals in the two regions is one hundred and forty, of which ninety - seven occur in Eurasia and seventy - five in North America. Of these, thirty - two are circumpolar, or common to both

[1] Allen, *Geographical Distribution of North American Animals*, 210.

regions; and out of the seventy - five in America only twenty - seven, a trifle over one - third, are peculiarly American. The most interesting result, however, appears in the comparison of the corresponding sub-regions of the two continents. Of forty-three genera in the North American cold temperate sub-region, six are common to both cold and warm, and seventeen are limited to the warm sub-region.[1] The general result, then, of the faunal comparison of the two continents is that the arctic faunas exhibit no difference, the north temperate sub-regions very little, and that specific differentiation increases rapidly as we pass southward. It may be well to recall that the comparison deals with genera; the great majority of species in both continents are of course peculiar.

The North American tropical region has sixty-two genera of mammals, and the fauna is widely divergent from that of the tropical regions of the Old World. The most characteristic mammals are the ant-eater, armadillo, sloth, tapir, peccary, jaguar, marmoset, and spider-monkey.

Proceeding to a consideration of the animals themselves in their relations to man, we shall notice such animals as are of economic importance, as sources of food, clothing, or other necessities; and the group which pre-eminently serves these functions is the ruminants. Of these the family which, all things

---

[1] It is an interesting fact that the majority of these peculiarly American genera are rodents.

considered, has been of most service to man is the
deer, of which the most significant is the Virginia
or white-tailed deer, which in some of its eight or
more sub-species and varieties inhabits nearly all
of the warm temperate sub-region.   It was the first
deer discovered by the early settlers; and to them
as well as to the Indians it was a staple source of
food and clothing.   It is the most adaptable and
the most abundant American deer, and will undoubtedly survive all other members of its family.
Essentially a lover of the forest, it avoids the arid
plains and high mountains of the northwest.   A
near relative of the white-tail is the mule-deer, sometimes called the black-tailed deer, which inhabits
the Bad Lands, and the foot-hills of the Rocky
Mountains.   This species bids fair to be exterminated in a few years owing to indiscriminate slaughter at all seasons.[1]

Of all the larger game animals, excepting only
the bison, the American elk or wapiti (*Cervus
canadensis*) has come the nearest to extermination.
Originally the species ranged through the Adirondack
and Alleghany mountains northward into Canada,
from the Great Lakes to Vancouver, and through
the Rocky Mountain region from Canada to Mexico.
In the eighteenth century elk were still plentiful
in the Alleghanies, and one was killed in central

[1] The name black-tailed deer should be restricted to the
Columbia black-tail of the Pacific coast, a variety of which,
the Sitka deer. extends northward into Alaska.

Pennsylvania as late as 1869. Now virtually extinct east of the Mississippi, the range of the elk is practically limited to the eastern slope of the Rockies, especially in western Colorado, Wyoming, and Montana, with a few representing local varieties in the Olympic Mountains of Washington and in Arizona and New Mexico. The present focus of the elk range is the Yellowstone Park, which forms a breeding-ground and summer nursery for a herd of twenty thousand head.

The moose (*Alces americanus*), the largest and most powerful of the deer family, has suffered much less than has the elk from the inroads of civilization. Its present range is from the Atlantic to the Pacific, through the wooded north temperate sub-region, especially in New Brunswick, Manitoba, Alberta, British Columbia, and Alaska,[1] and extending into the United States in Maine, northern Minnesota, and in the Rockies as far south as northern Wyoming. In the Adirondacks it was exterminated about 1860. While the number of moose has undoubtedly been sadly lessened by hunters, opinion differs as to the danger of its extinction. Though yielding the southern limit of their range, there is reason to believe that they are encroaching, perhaps to an equal extent, upon new forest lands to the northward. In certain parts of British Columbia and Alaska the dying out of the Indian tribes has

---

[1] The Alaska moose is generally regarded as a distinct species, *Alces gigas*.

allowed the moose to become much more numerous.

The caribou (*rangifer*), of which there are some seven fairly distinct varieties, falls within two main groups: the woodland caribou, which inhabits the wooded portion of British America extending into Maine and Montana; and the barren-ground caribou, which traverses the vast treeless tundras of arctic America and Greenland. The caribou is migratory and travels in immense herds, and being easy to kill it is slaughtered in great numbers by Eskimos and Indians. In some parts of Alaska it has been almost exterminated by natives, who have butchered them to sell the flesh to the whalers wintering on the coast. The final extinction of the caribou, however, is fortunately far distant.

Of all our ruminants, the one distinctive American, the one form which has no Old-World double, is the prong-horn antelope, which, zoologically, is intermediate between the deer and the bovidæ, or cattle. Formerly very abundant between the Missouri River and the Pacific coast, it now exists only on the great plains and the high plateaus, where its numbers are decreasing.

Of less actual value to civilized man than the above-mentioned species, but formerly very important to the Indians, are the mountain-sheep, or big-horn, and the Rocky Mountain goat. The former, once very abundant, is now limited to small bands, and is doomed to early extinction. The Rocky

Mountain goat, which is comparatively valueless for flesh or skin, ranges the higher Rocky and Cascade mountains from Montana to Alaska.

The musk-ox is a truly arctic form, originally circumpolar in distribution, but now restricted to the Western Hemisphere, where it ranges the frozen wastes of the barren grounds. A closely allied species has recently been discovered in Greenland. The long, woolly coat is highly valued by the Eskimos, and the flesh is said to be excellent. Quite recently the musk-ox has been extensively hunted by sportsmen.

Beyond all doubt the most noteworthy of all North American animals is the bison, or "buffalo," by reason of its majestic size, former countless numbers, its practical value, and its lamentable extermination. Originally the bison ranged from the Alleghanies to the Rockies and even farther west into Oregon and Nevada, and from Great Slave Lake southward nearly to central Mexico. By 1800 the species was practically exterminated east of the Mississippi, and by the middle of the century the buffalo were restricted to the great plains, where they continued to roam by millions, until 1869, when the completion of the Union Pacific Railway divided them into a "northern herd" and a "southern herd," and initiated the beginning of the end of the race. Previous to this time the killing had been desultory, but in 1871 began the systematic slaughter of the southern herd, which at

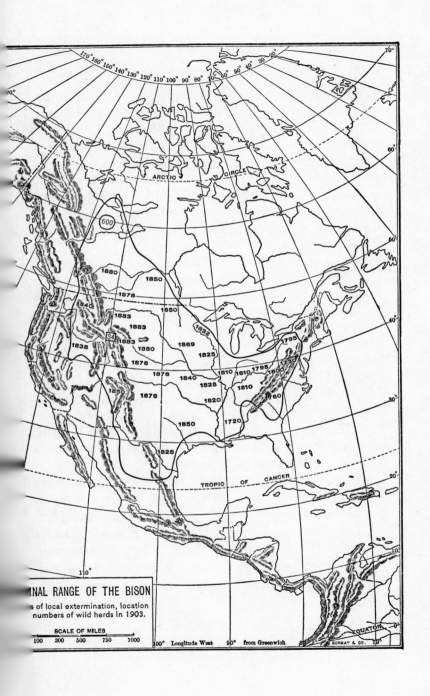

170° 160° 150° 140° 130° 120° 110° 100° 90° 80°   70° 60° 50° 40° 30° 20°

70°

ARCTIC   CIRCLE

60°

600

1880   1850

1878

1840   1850
1883
1883   1832
34   1883   1795
1838   1880   30
1876   1795
1876   1840   1810 1810 1795 1800
1825   1810
1850   1876   1820   1760
1850   1720
1828

TROPIC   OF   CANCER

110°

EQUATOR

NAL RANGE OF THE BISON

s of local extermination, location
numbers of wild herds in 1903.

SCALE OF MILES
100   300   500   750   1000

100° Longitude West   90°   from Greenwich   80°
BORMAY & CO.

that time numbered between three and four million, yet by 1876 was exterminated by the hide hunters. The opening of the Northern Pacific Railway in 1880 marked the beginning of a similar war of extermination of the northern herd, which contained one million five hundred thousand head; and by 1883 the end was accomplished and the sole survivors were some two hundred head in Yellowstone Park, five hundred and fifty near Great Slave Lake, and a few scattered smaller bands.[1] The Yellowstone herd has been sadly decimated by poachers, and in March, 1893, numbered thirty-four head, while the Canadian wild herd near Great Slave Lake contained about six hundred. Formerly completely intergraded with the southern form, the Canadian herd is now regarded as sufficiently distinct to warrant its designation as a variety—the wood bison. The buffalo in the various parks and private game preserves number about one thousand, and these are slowly increasing.

Regarding the former value of the buffalo to man, it is impossible to estimate closely the commercial value of the beef and hides during the period of active slaughter, but it has been placed at from $15,000,000 to $20,000,000. However, the real value of the buffalo was not to the white man, but to the Indian tribes of the great plains. Besides the flesh—fresh, dried, and made into pemmican—there were the hide, which yielded tipi, clothing, bed-

---

[1] Hornaday, *The Extermination of the American Bison*, 437.

ding, and shield; the sinews, which gave thread, rope, and bow-string; and the bones and horns, which were fashioned into implements of various kinds.

Turning now to the fur-bearing animals, we find that these belong chiefly to the carnivora and the rodents. Though many are distributed over the entire continent, the fur-bearers as a rule inhabit the northerly regions, and a large proportion are of more or less aquatic habits. The larger carnivora, including the bear, wolf, and cougar, or puma, are far less important commercially as fur-bearers. From the economic stand-point these animals are rather to be regarded as nuisances, owing to their depredations among deer and other game animals, and even among cattle and sheep. Of all these the wolf is the worst offender.

We are likely to underestimate the importance of the fur-bearers as a factor in the progress of civilization, unless we consider that for two centuries and a half these animals have been chiefly responsible for the penetration of the forests by trappers and traders, in order to supply the demand of European markets. This exploitation of the furs was in the north due chiefly to the famous Hudson Bay Company, established in 1670; but as early as 1763 a fur-trading post was established on the present site of St. Louis, and continued to be of great importance for the trade until the middle of the nineteenth century.

Examination of the carefully kept statistics of

the London fur market for the last century gives
an idea of the vast importance of the trade. Excepting the seals, the most valuable fur-bearers belong to the Mustelidæ or weasel family, represented
by the weasel, mink, sable, badger, skunk, wolverine,
otter, and sea-otter. The fur-bearing rodents include the squirrel, hare, musk-rat, and beaver; but
the beaver, which originally inhabited almost all the
wooded valleys of North America, is now nearly
extinct, except in some parts of the Rocky Mountain
region. At the present day the musk-rat far out-
ranks all other rodents in importance; the number
of skins of that species marketed in 1900 exceeded
five million.[1]

In recent years the most important branch of the
fur industry has been the seal - fisheries of Alaskan
waters, widely known through international com-
plications arising out of efforts by the United States
government to protect the seals in the high-seas.
Ever since the discovery of the Pribyloff Islands in
1786 the fur seal (*Callorhinus*) has been ruthlessly
slaughtered, but it is of interest to note that since
1799, when the Russian-American Company was
formed, laws have existed for its protection. From
1870 to 1890 the seal-fisheries, carefully guarded,
gave a yearly yield of one hundred thousand skins.
About 1886 the destructive practice of pelagic seal-
ing (shooting the animals at sea during migration)
began on a large scale, and has resulted in sadly

[1] U. S. Fish Commission, *Report*, 1904.

decreasing their numbers, so that the Pribyloff Islands herd in 1903 numbered only about two hundred thousand seals, of which some sixty thousand were breeding females.

The most valuable of all aquatic furs is that of the sea-otter of the north Pacific coast, but the annual catch has dwindled during the past twenty years from five thousand to five hundred skins.[1]

Quite recently the walrus of the arctic waters of both oceans has been hunted for its skin, the chief use of which is in the manufacture of metal polishers and certain fancy articles; but on account of its arctic range the walrus is safe from extermination.

The manatee of the Florida rivers was threatened with extinction a few years ago owing to a "fad" for its skin, but this rare animal now enjoys rigorous legal protection. Among aquatic animals there is one reptile of considerable importance—namely, the alligator of the gulf states and of Mexico. In view of the fact that two hundred and eighty thousand skins are used annually, it is not surprising that the supply is becoming rapidly reduced.

The relation of bird-life to mankind is too large a subject to be more than briefly mentioned in these pages; it touches, first, game birds, and, secondly, insect-eating birds. Nearly all the native birds are diminishing in numbers, statistics indicating that

[1] U. S. Fish Commission, *Report*, 1904.

the decrease during the last fifteen years has been forty per cent., and this is due, perhaps, as much to destruction of forests as to hunters. A number of species are now virtually extinct, the most notable being the passenger-pigeon which fifty years ago was common in flocks numbering millions. The wild turkey and the prairie-chicken are probably doomed, and only by strict reinforcement of the game laws can the various grouse, quail, and other game birds long survive. One bird of real value to man is the willow-ptarmigan of the frozen north, which is an important source of food to the Indians and Eskimos.

From an economic stand-point the most important wild creatures are the fishes, and of these the salmon of the north Pacific coast is easily in the lead. In 1899 the catch of salmon on that coast was nearly two hundred and fifty million pounds, with a value of over $10,000,000. These fish, fresh and dried, have long been the chief food staple of the Indians of the northwest coast. Next in importance is the cod of the Atlantic coast, the yearly catch of which in the United States alone is worth $3,000,000. Other important fishes of the Atlantic are the mackerel, herring, and alewife. A new branch of American industry is represented in the "sardine" fisheries of the Maine coast, which, though dating only from 1875, have an annual yield valued at $2,000,000. The "sardines" are chiefly young herring and several species related to the true sardine. The shad-fisheries of the Atlantic coast rivers are also among the most important. Of the fresh-water fishes the white-fish and lake herring, occurring chiefly in the Great Lakes, are the most important commercially.

CHAPTER V

ANTIQUITY OF MAN IN NORTH AMERICA

THE question as to how long man has lived upon the North American continent has been much discussed, and is still far from being satisfactorily answered. The attempts to prove by supposed finds of human remains and artifacts in suitable geological deposits that the continent was inhabited by man in pre-glacial or early glacial times, have thus far failed to produce conviction. Probably the most important evidence for such antiquity is ascribed to certain auriferous gravel beds in California. In 1866 in a mining shaft in Calaveras County in that state a skull was reported to have been found embedded in a deposit of gravel which geologists agree is of Tertiary age. Since that time other finds of human implements of various sorts have been reported from the same or similar deposits. If these objects were actually found where they were reported, the existence of Tertiary man in America may be regarded as established; and some well-known investigators have accepted this view.

More recent critical examination of the evidence,

however, has cast grave doubt on the authenticity of most of these so-called discoveries, and the general attitude to-day is one of decided scepticism. The chief objections to the evidence are as follows: the history of the finds is uncertain, it being even claimed that some of them were the results of practical jokes; in most cases the implements found are the same as those used by the Indians living in the vicinity, which are extremely common on the surface above the deposits; none of the objects show signs of having been subjected to the action of the violent torrents which formed the gravel beds; finally, some of the implements seem to be made of rock of more recent formations than the gravels themselves. Without going into further detail, it is enough to say that the presence of man in America at such an early date is extremely doubtful.[1]

In different places and at various times a considerable number of objects have been unearthed which have been claimed to prove the presence of man in the late glacial or early post-glacial period. These articles have been largely of chipped stone, many of them belonging to the so-called "palæolithic" class of implements. The most important of these finds were made in the valley of the Delaware River, in Ohio, and in Minnesota. The majority of them, under more critical examination, fail to be

[1] Holmes, " Preliminary Revision of the Evidence Relating to Auriferous Gravel Man in California " (*American Anthropologist*, N. S., I., 107–121, 614–645).

as convincing as at first appeared.   The possibilities
of intrusion from the surface are numerous, and
many of the implements under discussion are the
same as surface forms; while subsequent examination
by skilled observers, in places where objects were
claimed to have been found, have usually failed to
bring other specimens to light.   The result has been
that most archæologists regard the proof for glacial
man in America as insufficient.[1]   It must also be
added that the date of other deposits in which it is
generally agreed that human implements have been
found, such as the gravel series of Trenton, New
Jersey, has been placed by many investigators much
later than was at first supposed.[2]   Yet though
glacial man is doubtful, and there is little positive
foundation for a belief in such ancient occupation of
America as that of palæolithic man in Europe, the
continent has certainly been inhabited for a very
long period, probably for thousands of years.   Such
remains as some of those in Minnesota,[3] and a
recently discovered skull in Kansas,[4] prove a very
respectable antiquity.

[1] Mercer, *Researches upon the Antiquity of Man in the Delaware
Valley*, 20–33; Holmes, "Traces of Glacial Man in Ohio"
(*Journal of Geology*, I., 147–163.)

[2] General discussion of the Trenton gravels, Am. Assoc. Advancement of Science, *Proceedings* (1897), 344–390.

[3] Brower, *Memoirs of Exploration in the Basin of the Mississippi*, V.

[4] Holmes, "Fossil Human Remains Found Near Lansing,
Kansas" (*American Anthropologist*, N. S., IV., 743–752);
Chamberlin, "The Geologic Relations of the Human Relics of
Lansing, Kansas" (*Journal of Geology*, X., 745–779).

The study of cave deposits, which has led to such important conclusions in Europe, has produced negative results in America — instead of indicating great antiquity, caves explored in several states, both east and west, as well as in Mexico and South America, tend to prove the contrary. Careful examination of the hill - caves of Yucatan does not show the slightest trace of any ancient occupation, or of any other civilization than that found by the Spaniards upon their arrival in the country.[1]

Another set of problems relates to the so-called "mound-builders" and "cliff-dwellers." At present it seems to be fairly well agreed that these were no mysterious peoples who disappeared before the coming of the red man, but were merely the ancestors of the present American Indians. This does not necessarily imply that these structures were the work of the Indians inhabiting the particular regions when first discovered, though even that appears to have been the case in certain instances.

To appreciate this inquiry, let us briefly review some of the more important of the remains and antiquities which have thus far been discovered.

The archæological remains found in North America generally are unequally distributed and vary in different parts of the continent. In the arctic such records are not numerous, and consist principally of shell or refuse heaps, ruins of ancient stone houses, and numerous small objects such as are in

[1] Mercer, *The Hill-Caves of Yucatan.*

use by the Eskimo to - day. The houses are frequently found in regions no longer inhabited, and their presence in such places has been cited to support certain theories regarding Eskimo migration.[1]

In the eastern and central part of the continent, south of the arctic circle, appear a great number of remains which, while varying in details, yet show distinct relationship. Many classes of objects are limited in distribution, and indicate the existence of local cultural areas, or, if of wider occurrence, admit of classification into different groups. Yet archæological remains in general have so far not yielded sufficient material to permit the specification of definite prehistoric areas of culture; and many parts of the continent, particularly the western and south central states, have been examined very superficially or not at all, and the prehistoric records are practically unknown. Moreover, the same region may be, and has often been, occupied in successive periods by peoples of different types.

In view of the impossibility of any safe classification of human remains on the basis of the place of occurrence, we are forced to find some other classification, and a convenient one is a division into two groups: (1) local antiquities or monuments, including all objects which are fixed or stationary; (2) movable antiquities, including all the various relics

[1] Dall, " Tribes of the Extreme Northwest " (*Contributions to North American Ethnology*, I., pt. i.).

and remains of smaller size. Local antiquities may be subdivided into mounds, refuse-heaps, enclosures, hut-rings, excavations, mines and quarries, cave deposits, graves and cemeteries, garden-beds, bowlder effigies, hearths or camp sites, petroglyphs, and ancient trails.

Of these the mounds are perhaps the most important, certainly the most famous. They have been classified according to shape as conical, elongate, pyramidal, and effigy mounds. (a) The conical, which include most of the burial-mounds, are of all sizes up to eighty or ninety feet in height and three hundred feet in diameter. (b) The elongate mounds or walls, of unknown purpose, are from fifty to nine hundred feet in length, from ten to twenty feet in breadth, and are seldom more than four feet in height. (c) The pyramidal form differs from the conical chiefly in having a flat top, sometimes appearing like a mere earthen platform. Occasionally there are terraces on one or two sides, or a sort of roadway leading to the top. This type is found mainly in the lower Ohio Valley, Missouri, Arkansas, and the gulf states. It includes the two largest mounds known, the Cahokia, situated in Illinois, a few miles east of St. Louis, and the Etowah mound near Cartersville, Georgia. (d) The effigy mounds occur principally in Wisconsin and the adjacent parts of Illinois and Iowa, with a few in Ohio and Georgia. They are sometimes called emblematic or symbolic, but while some of them seem to have resemblances to animal forms, it is quite impossible to say what most of them were intended to represent. The most famous of these is probably the Serpent Mound, in Adams County, Ohio.[1]

Another important group of works falls under the term "enclosures." While pyramidal mounds usually occur on level lowlands, these enclosures are frequently found on bluffs and hill-tops, and are sometimes known as "hill forts" in consequence. Walls of earth and stone are also found thrown across necks of land, in the bends of rivers, on the shore-lines of lakes, or in the rear of projecting bluffs whose precipitous sides would afford protection from the attacks of enemies. The defensive purpose of many of these is evident enough, but in other cases their use is quite unknown. Fort Ancient, in Warren County, Ohio, may be regarded as the best example of these "hill forts."[2]

Other types of local antiquities need be referred to but briefly. In various parts of the country hundreds of rings of earth from five to fifteen feet in diameter, with the enclosed area more or less depressed, have been found. These are so obviously the remains of circular dwellings that they have been termed "hut-rings." In certain regions, notably in Arkansas, square house sites have been discovered, indicating at least a different if not a

[1] Putnam, "Serpent Mound of Ohio" (*Century Magazine*, April, 1890); Holmes, "The Serpent Mound" (*Science*, December 31, 1886).   [2] Moorehead, *Fort Ancient*.

more advanced type of culture. In connection with both varieties deposits of burned clay and ashes occur. The so-called "garden-beds," low, parallel ridges about six or eight inches high and four to ten feet apart, are chiefly found in Michigan and Wisconsin, but their significance is unknown.

Mines and quarries are found in innumerable places, and in their neighborhood there are often the "workshops" where the rough material was further worked over. At these quarries there are often great numbers of broken pieces, imperfect or defective specimens, rejects, etc., showing all stages of the process of manufacture from the first beginning up to the finished implement. The quarries and quarry workshops which are most common are those for the manufacture of flaked implements, such as arrow-points, spear-heads, stone knives, and the like. For this purpose bowlders of suitable rock, as, for example, quartzite, were sought, and the quarries are found where deposits of such bowlders or favorable rock occur. The implements were made by fracturing and chipping the rock into suitable shapes. Softer formations, such as steatite or soapstone, were quarried from massive deposits by means of picks and chisels of harder and tougher stone.[1] Copper

[1] Holmes, "Stone Implements of the Potomac - Tidewater Province" (Bureau of Ethnology, *Fifteenth Annual Report*); also two shorter papers by the same author—viz., "A Quarry Workshop of the Flaked Stone Implement Makers in the D. C." and "Excavations in an Ancient Soapstone Quarry in the D. C." (*American Anthropologist*, III., 1, 321).

was also mined by the aboriginal Americans, and the signs of their work are quite common in the Lake Superior copper district. The method was apparently simply to batter away the surrounding rock from the native metal with stone hammers.[1]

The investigation of these quarries and quarry workshops not only throws light on the methods of manufacture, but reveals the fact that many of the more roughly chipped specimens formerly regarded as crude implements and possible indications of palæolithic man may be nothing more than rejects or imperfect or only partly finished implements. As the rocks found in different localities often show marked variation, a careful study of the distribution of the different artifacts might throw much light on the early lines of travel and intercommunication.

Perhaps as important a class of remains as any other are the burial-mounds, graves, and cemeteries, for these yield not only skeletons but also the greater portion of the movable remains — the vessels, implements, and ornaments, which reveal at least something of the art and culture of the former inhabitants of the different regions. The shell mounds of the southern states have also been

[1] Whittlesey, *Ancient Mining on the Shores of Lake Superior* (Smithsonian *Contributions to Knowledge*, XIII., No. 155); Packard, "Pre-Columbian Copper Mining in North America" (Smithsonian Institution, *Report*, 1892, pp. 175–198); Holmes, "Aboriginal Copper Mines of Isle Royale" (*American Anthropologist*, N. S., III., 684–696).

the source of large collections of objects of significance.

The comparative study of some of the finds from these deposits has already proven of value.[1] For example, the pottery of the area east of the Mississippi seems to show but slight resemblance in character to that of other regions. In decorative designs there seem to be similarities between the southeast, particularly Florida, and the West Indies, making a certain interchange of culture elements highly probable. There are also traces of Yucatan influences on the gulf coast of the Florida peninsula.

Another interesting set of objects is represented by articles and ornaments of shell. The shell gorgets in particular show elaborate designs, some of them bearing such strong resemblance to Mexican art that it is difficult to regard it as the result of chance. Numerous articles of beaten copper, such as axes, spindles, disks, ear-pendants, rings, bracelets, etc., have also come to light, particularly in the shell mounds of Florida, and also in Ohio and Georgia. They have excited no little discussion as to whether they represent truly aboriginal workmanship or not, the majority of investigators apparently thinking that there is no good evidence of European influence.[2] A few objects beaten out

[1] Holmes, "Aboriginal Pottery of the Eastern United States" (Bureau of Ethnology, *Twentieth Annual Report*).

[2] Cf. discussion on the subject by C. B. Moore et al., in *American Anthropologist*, N. S., V., 27–57.

of native silver and gold or meteoric iron have also been found. It cannot be shown that any of these metals were ever smelted from the ore, though copper and the precious metals were sometimes cast in ancient Mexico. All iron objects which have been found, except the few of meteoric iron, are of European manufacture.

Of all prehistoric remains, stone objects are the most common; and together with pottery form the bulk of archæological collections. This is due in large part to their resistance to destructive agencies, for objects of wood and vegetable materials decay rapidly, and even bone objects are preserved only under favorable conditions. Among the most important classes of stone objects are the few human images discovered, mainly in Georgia, Tennessee, and southern Illinois. They all exhibit considerable similarity, varying in size from a few inches to over a foot in height.[1] Another interesting group of objects are supposed to have been used for ceremonial purposes. They are finely finished and polished, as a rule, and were made of various kinds of stone, slate being the favorite material. They include such objects as "banner stones," bird or saddle stones, boat-shaped implements, etc.

Weapons in great variety, such as arrow-points, spear-heads, knives, axes, celts, etc., form a large group and have been divided into numerous classes,

[1] Thomas, " Stone Images from Mounds and Ancient Graves " (*American Anthropologist*, IX., 404–408).

mainly according to form. Tools of many kinds
exist in great numbers, such as hammers, gouges,
scrapers, drills, adzes, chisels, and knives; and also
utensils, such as soapstone vessels, mortars and pes-
tles, in great variety. Pipes carved out of stone are
not at all uncommon and often show fine workmanship. Among ornaments and miscellaneous objects
may be mentioned pendants, beads, disks, plummets
or sinkers, and many other articles the use of which
is not known.[1]

For the now generally accepted belief that the
makers of all these various objects were none other
than the ancestors of the present Indians there
are several reasons. In the first place, the general
culture revealed by the remains is practically the
same as that of the Indians before they were
modified by contact with the whites. Moreover,
the early explorers found mounds used as sites for
dwellings; and not only ascribe their construction
to the Indians, but describe the methods by which
they were built.[2] Fortifications are also known
to have been erected and used by the Indians.
Additional evidence comes from the mounds themselves, since iron objects and articles of undoubted
European manufacture have been found in a number
of them, showing that some at least were constructed

---

[1] The literature on stone implements and objects is voluminous.
A general work with many references is Moorehead, *Prehistoric
Implements: A Reference Book*.

[2] Thomas, *American Archæology*, chap. x.

since the advent of Europeans. Yet in some regions, as Ohio, where some of the most important of these structures are found, there is good reason for thinking that their construction was not due to any tribe known to have inhabited the region within historic times. Some writers ascribed their origin to the Cherokees, who have traditions to that effect, but this conclusion is doubtful. In any case the culture exhibited in the mounds is not beyond that of many Indian tribes; and the theory of a pre-Indian race of mound-builders is unnecessary, and brings in the difficulty of accounting for the total disappearance of such a race.

Turning now to the western portion of the continent we find, outside of Mexico, several well-marked cultural areas, of which it will be sufficient to mention the northwest coast, California, and the pueblo region. The archæology of the north Pacific region is closely connected with the present inhabitants of that section, who will be described below.[1] In California, especially to the south, but little is known of the culture of the aboriginal inhabitants, who seem to have readily yielded to the teachings of the early Spanish missionaries and rapidly dwindled under their care. On the coast and islands of southern California some very in-

---

[1] Smith, *Archæology of Lytton*, B. C. (Am. Mus. Nat. Hist., *Memoirs*, 1899); *Archæology of the Thompson River Region, B. C. (ibid.*, 1900); *Shell Heaps of the Lower Fraser River, B. C. (ibid.*, 1903).

teresting finds have been made, especially of stone
articles. Pottery seems to have been unknown in
this region until after the coming of the Spaniards.[1]

In the pueblo region, however, most remarkable
remains have been found. High up on the sides of
many of the numerous cañons of this section were
discovered the ruins of old stone buildings containing from a single room to more than a hundred,
and sometimes three or four stories high. The
largest of these, known as Cliff Palace, is estimated
to have one hundred and twenty - five rooms on the
ground floor alone. These structures are perched
on lofty and almost inaccessible ledges or shelves
along the walls of the cañons, and are protected by
the overhanging cliffs above. They are especially
numerous in the region of the Mesa Verde, in southwestern Colorado, but are found in many of the
neighboring cañons, and even in the region west
of the Colorado and in northern Mexico. As they
are well protected by recesses in the cañon wall,
not only the stone-work, but the wooden beams of
the floors between the different stories are well preserved. On examination these ruins have yielded
a large number of interesting objects. Among
them may be enumerated several skeletons, one
wrapped in a kind of feather cloth, others in mat-

[1] Gates, *Prehistoric Man in California;* Gates, in Moorehead,
Prehistoric Implements, 230–252; also reports by F. W. Putnam
et al., in U. S. *Geographical Surveys West of the 100th Meridian*,
VII. (*Archæology*).

ting; cotton cloth, mats and baskets of osiers; sandals of yucca leaves and cords of yucca fibres; pottery of various types; numerous objects of stone, bone, and wood; also corn, both shelled and on the cob, and beans. The wooden articles and textile fabrics were remarkably well preserved.[1]

In addition to the cliff dwellings, which are merely stone houses built on protected ledges, cave dwellings and artificial cavate abodes are also found. These occur chiefly on the west side of the Rio Grande, between Santa Clara and Cochiti, and in the upper San Juan Valley. In some cases these seem to have been cut out of the solid rock, usually a soft volcanic tufa or shale.[2]

On the plateaus and in the valleys of the southwest ruins of stone buildings are quite common as far west as the one hundred and thirteenth meridian; those which have been most thoroughly examined are chiefly in the drainage area of the San Juan River. Many of these structures have probably been inhabited within historic times; others were doubtless in ruins when the Spaniards first arrived. Some of the largest and most remarkable are situated in the Chaco Cañon; one of these, known as Pueblo Bonito, is roughly semicircular in

[1] Nordenskiold, *The Cliff Dwellers of the Mesa Verde;* Birdsall, "The Cliff Dwellings of the Cañons of the Mesa Verde" (Am. Geog. Soc., *Bulletin*, XXIII., 584–620).

[2] Holmes, *Report on the Ancient Ruins of Southwestern Colorado, Examined in 1875 and 1876;* U. S. Geol. and Geog. Survey of the Territories, *Tenth Report*, 388.

outline and about five hundred and thirty feet in length by three hundred and eight in width. The rooms are arranged around a central court, being five or six deep in the curved portion and doubtless several stories high next the outer wall. The whole arrangement was evidently for protection from enemies, as in the case of some of the modern pueblos.

In the Gila Valley are numerous adobe ruins, Casa Grande being the best known.[1] In this region are also found large ditches and remains of a former system of irrigation, by which it is estimated that at least two hundred and fifty thousand acres could be supplied.[2] In northern Mexico, in the western part of the state of Chihuahua, are several ruins similar to those of the Gila valley, known as Casas Grandes, or "Great Houses." The culture of their inhabitants seems to have been somewhat higher than that of the more northern pueblos, as indicated by certain household utensils, the possible existence of stairways in the interior of the houses, and by the method of constructing irrigation ditches.[3]

Who were the builders of these old ruins? With regard to the cliff dwellings in particular many

[1] Mindeleff, "Casa Grande Ruin" (Bureau of Ethnology, *Thirteenth Annual Report*, 289–319).

[2] Hodge, "Prehistoric Irrigation in Arizona" (*American Anthropologist*, VI., 323–330).

[3] Bandelier, *Final Report of Investigations Among the Indians of the Southwestern U. S.;* Archæological Institute of America, *Papers American Series*, IV., 569.

theories have been advanced. The idea of a distinct cliff-dwelling race, which has since entirely disappeared, has been generally discarded, and it is now generally believed that part of the buildings at least were constructed and used by the ancestors of some of the present Pueblo Indians; perhaps some of them were built by the ancestors of the present Navajos.[1]

That some of these structures were occupied during historic times[2] is made probable by the traditions of some of the neighboring tribes. Certain of the Hopi clans claim to have lived at Cañon de Chelly;[3] others on the upper Rio Grande, in the Gila Valley.[4] The possible accuracy of such legends is illustrated by the discussion which arose recently over the claim of the Acoma Indians to have once lived on the "Enchanted Mesa," in which their tradition was fully supported[5] by investigation. On the other hand, there is historical evidence that some of the pueblos were deserted and in ruins at the time of Coronado's expedition in 1540.[6]

[1] Hodge, "The Early Navajo and Apache," in American Anthropologist, VIII., 239.
[2] Mindeleff, "Cliff Ruins of Cañon de Chelly, Arizona" (Bureau of Ethnology, Sixteenth Annual Report), 162, 163.
[3] Ibid., 191.
[4] Fewkes, "Tusayan Migration Legends" (Bureau of American Ethnology, Nineteenth Annual Report, pt. ii., 573–634).
[5] Hodge, "The Enchanted Mesa," in National Geographic Magazine, VIII., 273–284).
[6] Report of Hernando de Alvarado, in Winship, "The Coronado Expedition" (Bureau of Ethnology, Fourteenth Annual Report, pt. i., 594).

Hand-in-hand with the question of the antiquity of man on the continent goes the problem of whence he came. Unfortunately, this important question must be answered by the admission that the only conservative and defensible position at the present day is one of frank ignorance. Theories of Asiatic, European, African, or Polynesian origin are all equally dangerous and weak. Geological solutions by lost Atlantises and former land bridges from the Old World may be invoked, but convince nobody except their proposers. The thorough ethnological studies which are now under way may at some time in the future throw light upon the problem; and we have arrived at the point of assurance that, in the past, northwestern America and northeastern Asia formed one area of culture. Whether that of the west came from the east, or that of the east was derived from the west, it is as yet impossible to say.[1]

[1] Bogoras, in *American Anthropologist*, N. S., IV. (1902), 577. Cf. also the Jesup North Pacific Expedition Reports (Am. Mus. of Nat. Hist., *Memoirs*, 1898–1904).

CHAPTER VI

CLASSIFICATION AND DISTRIBUTION OF THE
AMERICAN INDIANS

(1500–1900)

THOUGH there is no universally accepted scheme of classification of the native races of America, their essential unity is always recognized. Viewed broadly, their racial relations are closer to the Mongoloid type of man than to any other. But even essential unity allows wide variation in details, and Nature has seized her privilege in producing the existing confusion of Indian stocks. Anthropologists of to-day determine groups on one of four sets of characteristics—physical, linguistic, geographical, and general culture. The first two criteria are the more exact, and the linguistic classification of North American tribes has been accepted as the most satisfactory for scientific study. The latter two criteria are the more convenient and sometimes the only feasible bases of classification. Hence, for the purposes of this volume, a combination of the geographical and cultural will be followed. Nevertheless, it must never be forgotten that the limits of physical, linguistic, and cultural groups do not correspond; and the overlapping of stocks determined by those criteria is an unavoidable complication.

The physical characteristics of the American race are difficult to formulate in general terms. The Indian is, however, as a rule, of fairly high stature, five feet eight or ten inches, though undersized in certain groups, notably in the far north and in the extreme south. On the other hand, he has a very tall stature, six feet or over, in some groups, such as the prairie tribes of North America, and certain peoples of the Amazon basin and of Patagonia in the southern continent.

The hair is almost invariably black, coarse, long, and straight on the head, and scanty on the face and body. The smooth face of the male Indian is often due, however, to the almost universal practice of extracting the beard by the roots.

The color of the skin is of all shades of brown, ranging from a relatively dark complexion in the uplands to a light yellowish in certain woodland stocks. The so-called "Red Indian" does not exist. The early observers saw Indians painted red, and perhaps a reddish tone was present in the skin of the eastern woodland stocks with which European immigrants first came into contact. In the vast majority of the Indians no such tint is discernible.

The shape of the skull is neither decidedly dolichocephalic nor brachycephalic except in special extreme instances, but in general is of the mesocephalic type. The Eskimo, however, are one of the longest-headed races on the earth, and certain stocks both in North and South America are markedly broad-headed. The custom of deforming the heads of new-born children by artificial pressure has produced some extreme types, which, however, have no biological significance.

The cheek-bones are usually prominent, but with lateral rather than high projection; in some regions this feature is not evident. The nose is usually large and prominent; it is often aquiline, but in certain groups, particularly among the tribes of the northwest coast, it is short and has a tendency to flatness. The eyes are very dark and usually rather small. In the northwest the oblique eye often appears, and the same tendency is seen in the children of many stocks even when it is not evident in the adult.

All these characteristics are fairly general, particularly in North America, but variations sufficient to form recognizable types are not infrequent. For example, the short, squat Eskimo, with Mongoloid features and light skin, is strikingly different from the tall, dark, impressive Sioux or Algonkin; and the coarse-faced Indian of Puget Sound is easily distinguished from the more delicately featured native of the southwest.

As has been stated above, linguistic characteristics have proven the most trustworthy basis for grouping the vast number of tribes of the northern continent. The languages of North America in general are highly agglutinative. Suffixes, prefixes, and parts of speech are added to the verb to a bewildering degree, and all the terms of any sentence tend to be brought together into a single word, in most cases the verb with which subject and object have been incorporated. These common characteristics do not prevent, however, a very wide diversity, not only in the vocabularies, but in the structures and morphologies of the different American languages.

Much attention has been and is being given to the analysis of the Indian tongues. Tentative classifications of linguistic families have been made, based upon inspection and comparison of vocabularies, and fortunately are for the most part sustained by comparisons based on syntax. When such comparison shows that the resemblances between two languages are not sufficient to indicate a common origin or undeniable relation, the two groups are regarded as independent stocks or families. The exact number of such stocks in North America it is at present impossible to state, but it is probably about seventy-five. It must be remembered that each of these stocks may, and in most cases does, speak many dialects so different as to be mutually unintelligible, even though grammatically related. The distribution of stock languages also varies widely, some extending nearly across the continent and embracing hundreds of divisions, while others are confined to a few square miles and are spoken by a handful of survivors.

The Bureau of Ethnology[1] in Washington has determined fifty-nine independent linguistic families north of Mexico, and with certain slight modifications we may accept this as the best classification at our disposal. The distribution of these stocks when first met by Europeans is shown in the accompanying map reproduced from a report of the bureau. To avoid confusion, the termination "an" or "ian" has been given to the family name to distinguish it from a merely tribal designation; but wherever possible the name for the family has been derived from that of one of its tribes, a convenient method though it gives rise to some unwieldy terms. It must also be remembered that most of the tribes and stocks have been described in literature under many different names, and as a consequence the common designation is often very different from the technical. These discrepancies will so far as possible be made clear in subsequent chapters. The stocks with their most important constituent tribes, according to the classification of the Bureau of Ethnology, are as follows:

Algonquian family.—Principal tribes: Abnaki, Algonkin, Arapaho, Cheyenne, Conoy, Cree, Delaware (Lenape), Fox, Illinois, Kickapoo, Massachuset, Menominee, Miami, Micmac, Mohegan, Montagnais,

[1] Powell, " Indian Linguistic Families " (Bureau of Ethnology, *Seventh Annual Report*, 1891).

Montauk, Munsee, Nanticoke, Narraganset, Nauset, Nipmuc, Ojibwa, Ottawa, Pamlico, Pennacook, Pequot, Piankishaw, Pottawotomi, Powhatan, Sauk, Shawnee, Siksika (Blackfoot), Wampanoag, Wappinger.

Athapascan family.—Principal tribes: Northern group—Ahtena, Chippewyan, Kenai, Kuchin, Loucheux, Nahauni, Sarcee, Sicauni, Slave, Taculli. Pacific group—Chasta, Chetco, Hupa, Rogue River (various tribes), Umpqua. Southern group—Apache, Aricaipa, Chiracahua, Coyotero, Jicarilla, Lipan, Mescalero, Navajo.

Attacapan family.

Beothukan family.

Caddoan family. — Principal tribes: Adaize, Arikara, Caddo, Pawnee, Wichita. ,

Chimakuan family.—Principal tribes: Chimakum, Quileute.

Chimarikan family.

Chimmesyan family.—Principal tribes: Nasqua, Tsimshian.

Chinookan family.—Principal tribes: Lower Chinook group—Chinook, Clatsop. Upper Chinook group—Cathlamet, Clackama, Multnoma, Wahkiacum, Wasco.

Chitimachan family.

Chumashan family.

Coahuiltecan family.

Copehan family.

Costanoan family.

Eskimauan family.—Principal tribes and villages may be classified in groups as follows: Greenland, Labrador, Central, Alaskan, Aleutian, Asiatic.

Esselenian family.

Iroquoian family.—Principal tribes: Cayuga, Cherokee, Conestoga, Erie, Mohawk, Neuter, Nottoway, Oneida, Onondaga, Seneca, Tionontate, Tuscarora, Wyandot.

Kalapooian family.

Karankawan family.

Keresan family.

Kiowan family.

Kitunahan family. — Principal tribes: Upper, Lower, and Flathead Kootenay.

Koluschan family.—Principal tribes: Chilcat, Sitka, Yakutat, etc., usually grouped under name Tlingit.

Kulanapan family.

Kusan family.

Lutuamian family.—Principal tribes: Klamath and Modoc.

Mariposan family.

Moquelumnan family.

Muskhogean family.—Principal tribes: Alabama, Apalachi, Chickasaw, Choctaw, Creek or Maskoki, and Seminole.

Natchesan family.

Palaihnihan family.

Piman family.

Pujunan family.

Quoratean family.

Salinan family.

Salishan family.—Principal tribes: Bellacoola, Chehalis, Clallam, Colville, Cowlitz, Okinagan, Puyallup, Quinault, Shuswap, Skokomish, Snohomish, Spokan, Thompson, Tillamook.

Sastean family.

Shahaptian family.—Principal tribes: Nez Percé (Chopunnish), Klikitat, Paloos, Tenaino, Umatilla, Walla Walla.

Shoshonean family.—Principal tribes: Bannock, Comanche, Paiute, Shoshone, Tusayan, Ute.

Siouan family.—Principal groups and tribes: Dakota group, including Santee, Sisseton, Wahpeton, Yankton, Yanktonnais, and Teton (Brule, Ogalalla, Uncpapa, etc.), Assinaboin, Omaha, Ponca, Kaw, Osage, Quapaw, Iowa, Otoe, Missouri, Winnebago, Mandan, Gros Ventre, Crow, Tutelo, Biloxi, Catawba, Woccon.

Skittagetan family.—Principal tribes: Haida, Kaigani.

Takilman family.

Tañoan family.

Timuquanan family.

Tonikan family.

Tonkawan family.

Uchean family.

Waiilatpuan family.—Principal tribes: Cayuse, Molale.

Wakashan family.—Principal groups: Aht and Haeltzuk divisions.

Washoan family.
Weitspekan family.
Wishoskan family.
Yakonan family.
Yanan family.
Yukian family.
Yuman family.
Zuñian family.

It must not be supposed that the list given above is final, for it is quite possible that modifications will result from more complete linguistic knowledge; but it is evident to-day that such changes will not be fundamental, and the classification as it stands is a splendid achievement.

The distribution of the families as shown by the map suggests several points of interest. It will be seen that in most cases the stocks occupy continuous areas, which argues strongly for the view that the Indians at the time of the arrival of the Europeans were mainly stationary; that is, were not nomadic, for of course movements and campaigns of greater or less extent were taking place constantly. On the other hand, such a dispersion as that exhibited by the Athapascan stock, with its two great bodies, one in the extreme north and the other on the Mexican border, indicates earlier migration of great magnitude: it could not have been recent, for there has been time for the dialects to become widely differentiated and for the cultures to change with the environments, until there are few phases to be recognized as common. Similar, but less striking, dispersions are to be seen in the Siouan, Algonquian, Iroquoian, Shoshonean, and other families.

In speculating as to times and periods of separation, it must be remembered that these linguistic differences between families are not dialectic but fundamental; and the length of time necessary to effect such developments is staggering to contemplate. From the nature of the evidence our knowledge of the prehistoric migrations can never be exact. Physiographic features, doubtless, determined the direction of the movements in a majority of cases, and linguistic and archæological information tends to support that view. What particular inducement or pressure may have caused the Athapascan and other dispersions it is impossible to say; but the course of the movements can sometimes be inferred. The Athapascan movement was probably from the north southward along the plateaus or the great plains to the Mexican border; and subsequent pressure from the east pushed a number of the family representatives westward to the Pacific coast, where, cut off and isolated, they form the scattered intrusions which have long puzzled the students of American ethnology. The original habitat of the Siouan stock was certainly in the east, and there is fair evidence that it was found in the southeastern states between the Alleghanies and the sea. The Siouan occupancy of the Ohio Valley was not long antecedent to the coming of the whites; and the later extension over the northern plains was within historic times. Several small remnants were left behind by the Sioux and became known to the Europeans as the Catawba, Tutelo, Biloxi, and other tribes of the family in the Carolinas and the gulf states. This family in its migrations came early into collision with the westward movement of the Algonquian stock, chiefly represented by the powerful group of the Ojibwa, who in common with the other eastern families were being subjected to severe pressure at the hands of the Iroquois.

With regard to the Algonquian migrations all evidence points to the north Atlantic region as the centre from which the southern and western extension proceeded. The original Iroquoian home was probably the lower St. Lawrence, whence they were driven west and south by Algonquian hostility. The date of the breaking away of the Cherokee, their largest tribe and most southern representative, is entirely unknown, but in view of the linguistic differentiation it must have been at a very early period. The other tribes of the family were found on the lower St. Lawrence by the French in 1535, and their expulsion by the Algonquians was subsequent to that date. The formation of the Iroquois league profoundly modified the movements of the two stocks of the region. The direction of the Shoshonean dispersion is difficult to infer. The representatives in the United States would appear to have moved southward along the plateaus and diverged into southern California and the pueblo region of the southwest. Many competent authorities regard the Aztec or Nahua as a branch of this family; and if so, the movement may have been primarily northward with a subsequent return.

While these great movements had doubtless been in progress for many centuries, and were going on at the time of the discovery, the evidence is in favor of relative fixity of residence. The Indians were not nomadic, but occupied well-defined areas, with sparsely settled territories between the groups.

The number of the aborigines has been absurdly over-estimated.[1] Clearly, when the whites first appeared the population was very small in proportion to the enormous territory which it occupied. The density of the population varied greatly with the character of the country and the food supply; and inferences with regard to the peopling of untravelled parts of the continent, from observations on the regions first visited by Europeans, are extremely dangerous. Compilations of figures from the statements of early writers would indicate a population of somewhat under two hundred thousand for the territory east of the Mississippi, at the time of the discovery. The Pacific coast also undoubtedly sup-

[1] Mallery, "The Former and Present Number of Our Indians" (Am. Assoc. Advancement of Science, *Proceedings*, for 1877), p. 340; Powell, "Indian Linguistic Families" (Bureau of Ethnology, *Seventh Annual Report*, 33).

ported a numerous population, but the great intervening portion of the continent was probably thinly
peopled. It is not likely that the Indians north of
Mexico numbered much more than five hundred
thousand when the whites appeared. The decrease
during the four centuries that have elapsed since the
discovery, while not rapid, except in certain cases,
has nevertheless been constant.

The government statistics indicate a present
Indian population for the area named of something
less than four hundred thousand, but it must be
remembered that this enumeration includes a very
large proportion of mixed bloods. In certain regions
like the Pacific coast imperfect assimilation of
civilized methods of life and consequent unhygienic
conditions, coupled with the ravages of many
diseases of white introduction, are causing a rapid
decrease in the Indian population; and with the
death rate markedly higher than the birth rate, its
early extinction in that section is inevitable. In
other regions, such as the southwest, the Indian
seems to be more nearly holding his own, though
even there much of his apparent success in the
struggle is due to the inclusion of mixed bloods in
the census. In general, it is clear that he is slowly
but surely giving way. Statistics from Mexico are
scanty, but the indications are that the native
population in that country is not losing ground.

The map also brings out the fact that linguistic
and cultural limits do not coincide except in the

case of small families. Considering the extreme
variations in climate and general character which
the continent presents, it is not strange that widely
different cultures should obtain in different regions.
The shores of the Arctic Ocean and the deserts of the
southwest must necessarily produce sharp con-
trasts in the manner of life of the inhabitants;
and the same will be true for the forest-dwelling
tribes of the east and the Indians of the great
plains. For purposes of description it becomes
necessary to devise a grouping on a combined basis
of geographical distribution and general culture.
It is difficult if not impossible in dealing with the
complex psychological and social phenomena which
go to make up what we call culture, to lay down any
criteria for comparison which will be satisfactory in
all fields. What is characteristic in art may not
apply to religion; and the result of a comparison
in social organization will not hold in industrial life.

The only possible method of describing the Indian
tribes is to resort to a broad basis of generalization
which must, from the very nature of the subject, be
inexact in details. A classification which includes
considerations both of geography and culture, and
which seems open to less objection than any other,
is the following:

I. The Eskimo; II. The tribes of the north
Pacific coast; III. The tribes of the Mackenzie
River basin and the high plateaus; IV. The tribes
of the Columbia River and California; V. the tribes

of the plains; VI. the tribes of the eastern woodlands; VII. the tribes of the southwest and of
Mexico. It must not be inferred that these groups
all exhibit striking differences in every field, or that
further logical subdivision might not be made. It
will be noticed, however, that the groups suggested
correspond roughly to great specialized physical
areas of the continent; and they will be seen later
to possess some strongly marked cultural distinctions.

CHAPTER VII

THE ESKIMO AND THE NORTH PACIFIC INDIANS
(1500–1900)

THE word Eskimo is derived from the Abnaki dialect of the Algonquian and means "he eats raw flesh," a characterization quickly made by the southern neighbors of the group in question. The Eskimo themselves use the term *Innuit*, or "people," following the usual egotistical habit of primitive men in designating their own particular group. The distribution of the Eskimo is uniform and the cultural results are very significant and interesting. They are essentially a coast people and confined to the higher latitudes of the continent; and, notwithstanding the enormous separation and practical isolation of their constituent villages, the uniformity of their type, language, and culture is one of the most striking lessons of ethnography.

Their seat is the coast of North America from southern Labrador around the arctic shores to southern Alaska. Offshoots have pushed north to Smith Sound in Greenland and west across Bering Strait to Asia. Seldom ranging more than a few miles from the coast except on hunting expeditions, they seem to have held their undesirable foothold secure against all attacks from the interior. The earlier southern extension of the Eskimo has given rise to much discussion, conjecture, and assertion.[1] That they formerly occupied the Atlantic coast as far south as New England is not only possible but probable. That they ranged south of that territory is unlikely.

To the problem of the origin of the Eskimo, or, better, their point of dispersion, have been applied many vagaries of reasoning and guess. The favorite view has been that their origin was Asiatic, and that crossing Bering Strait they pushed along the arctic coast and down the Atlantic until apparently checked by counter influences. This idea, based on a popular preference for Asiatic beginnings, was strengthened by a superficial facial resemblance of the Eskimo to Mongoloid types, and later by the belief of some scientific authorities in a derivation from the early cave men of Europe.[2] This theory is founded upon very scanty material and equally loose ethnological reasoning. Without entering into the details of the controversy, there can be no doubt that the weight of authority to-day is not only in favor of considering the Eskimo as essentially American in type but also as American in origin, so far as origins can be traced at all. The

[1] Packard, in *American Naturalist*, 1885, p. 471.
[2] Dawkins, *Early Man in Britain*, 233; John Fiske, *Discovery of America*, 17.

prevailing view is that the primeval home or point of dispersion was somewhere south of Hudson's Bay; and that from there a migration in three directions took place—northeast into Labrador and Greenland, north to the shores of the arctic, and northwest to Alaska and Asia.[1]

As a rule, the Eskimo are undersized, but in the west, and notably in the Mackenzie River region, they are tall, muscular, and vigorous.[2] Their faces are very broad; noses fairly prominent; hair dark, usually black, and fairly abundant on the face; eyes dark brown or sometimes blue. The skin color ranges through all shades of brown, but is usually moderately dark. The skull is very dolichocephalic in most cases, but not invariably. Recent careful investigations of the brain development of the Eskimo indicate that it compares very favorably with that of Europeans.[3]

The Eskimo afford a capital example of the dependence of culture on environment. The climatic conditions deprive them of any considerable use of vegetable food or of the flesh of land animals, and they are forced to seek nutrition from the sea. Not alone for food, but to a great extent for clothing,

---

[1] Rink, *The Eskimo Tribes;* Boas, " The Central Eskimo " (Bureau of Ethnology, *Sixth Annual Report); Murdoch, in American Anthropologist,* 1888, p. 129.

[2] Petitot, *Vocabulaire Français-Esquimau,* 1876, p. xii.

[3] Hrdlicka, *An Eskimo Brain;* Spitzka, " Contributions to the Encephalic Anatomy of the Races " (*Am. Jour. of Anatomy,* II., 25).

fuel, and other necessities, they have made provision
with great ingenuity. Seal and walrus are their
staples—the meat for food, the fat for light and fuel,
the skins for clothing and protection, the bones
for the framework of canoes, etc. The popular
impression that the Eskimo live mainly upon blubber
and fat is entirely wrong, for that article is far too
precious and necessary for light and heat to be
wasted on food.

Their winter houses are built of blocks of packed
snow, in the form, roughly, of a hemisphere, and in-
volving the principle of the arch. Summer houses
are constructed of skins. One of the most interesting of Eskimo devices is the stone lamp in which
blubber oil is burned by means of a wick of moss.
The origin and distribution of the Eskimo lamp
have given rise to much discussion. It is held by
some that it was derived from the Scandinavians
in Greenland in comparatively recent times, and
thence spread rapidly from group to group until it
became one of the most distinctive of Eskimo
utensils. Other authorities regard it as entirely
an indigenous device.[1]

Next to the lamp, the development of the dog-
sledge and the skin canoe must be regarded as the
important factors in the industrial life of these people.
They are both admirably suited to their purposes and

[1] Tylor, in *Jour. Anthrop. Inst.*, 1884, p. 349; consult, also,
Hough, " The Origin and Range of the Eskimo Lamp," in
American Anthropologist, 1898, p. 118.

are usually adopted at once by whites or members of other tribes who come among them. The skill of the Eskimo hunter in handling his "kayak" in the pursuit of walrus and seal has become proverbial.

Eskimo decorative art exhibits striking variations, and is one of the phases of culture upon which much has been based in the theories of origin and distribution. In the eastern and central groups the art is rude and in places may hardly be said to exist. As one passes westward it becomes richer and richer, until in Alaska the carving and etching on bone and ivory and the work in basketry of the Aleutian Islanders are among the most beautiful examples of primitive æsthetic and technical production. In this connection, too, should be mentioned the passion for music and the facility in the composition of songs, which the Eskimo display. These songs are usually occasional or topical. Competitions in versification are frequent and are often used as a means of settling disputes and quarrels even of a serious nature, in which case the audience acts as judge.[1]

The religion of the Eskimo is animistic and much like that of all American peoples. Great numbers of spirits are believed to exist and to exert immediate influence upon human affairs. Dealings with these spirits are carried on chiefly through the shamans, usually known as "angekoks," who may be of either

[1] Cranz, *History of Greenland*, 178; Nansen, *First Crossing of Greenland*, 337.

sex. As a rule, one of the spirits is regarded as superior to all others, and in certain regions—*e. g.*, among the central Eskimo—this spirit is a woman. It is she who creates and transforms, who receives the souls of the dead; and it is to her that most of the ceremonials are devoted, and about her that the chief myths centre.

The social organization of the Eskimo is based on the immediate family, and no clan or gentile system is in use except in Alaska, where it has undoubtedly been derived from contact with Indians.[1] Marriage between those of recognized relationship is forbidden, and monogamy is the rule, though polygamy is permitted and common where the means of the husband are sufficient for the support of the additional families. A man's property usually descends to his eldest son, who is then bound to provide for his mother and younger brothers and sisters, or the same duty devolves upon whoever inherits. The group organization is in villages, and these are almost invariably small, usually not more than ten or fifteen huts. Chieftainship is conspicuous by its absence, though, as a matter of course, age, experience, and prowess wield an influence as great as though formally recognized.

The homogeneity of the Eskimo stock wherever found is its most salient feature. Notwithstanding the time which must have been consumed in the

---

[1] Nelson, "The Eskimo about Bering Strait" (Bureau of Ethnology, *Eighteenth Annual Report*, 322).

geographical dispersion of the race, even dialectic differences of speech are not to be compared with those which exist within most of the Indian linguistic families. An Eskimo from Labrador will within a very few weeks be able to communicate freely with a representative from Alaska, and the divergence is largely a matter of pronunciation and minor differences of vocabulary.[1]

Doubtless this cultural independence is very largely the result of the Eskimo's comparative isolation and freedom from contact with Indians. The only region where an intermixture of any moment takes place is in Alaska, and it is precisely there that the variations in custom and physical type appear most marked. The Aleutian branch of the Eskimo borders on the Tlingit Indian stock, and the mutual effect in physical type and in institutions is at once evident. A similar contact occurs in the case of the Eskimo of eastern Alaska and of the mouth of the Mackenzie River and the Athapascan tribes of the adjacent interior; and the same interchange of culture may be traced without difficulty.

Passing south from the Aleutian chain along the Pacific coast, the Eskimo characteristics grow rapidly fewer and soon disappear entirely. For purposes of description it is most convenient to group together all the coast tribes of Indians from Alaska to Vancouver Island. This does not mean that marked diversities are not present in the

[1] Brinton, *American Race*, 64.

culture of this extensive collection of tribes and stocks, but simply that the similarities are far more conspicuous than the differences. The leading tribes of this area are the Tlingit of Alaska; the Haida of Queen Charlotte Islands; the Tsimshian and Bella Coola of British Columbia; and the Heiltsuk group, of which the Kwakiutl of Vancouver Island is possibly the most important tribe.

Even physically these Indians are not homogeneous. Compared with those living east of the Rocky Mountains, they are shorter and have lighter skins. As was hinted above, in the most northern of this group of tribes we find certain superficial resemblances to the Eskimo type: the face is very broad but short, and the nose is straight or concave and is but slightly elevated, which gives the features a Mongoloid cast. The eyes are not, however, except in a few cases, noticeably oblique. Among the more southerly tribes of the group in the neighborhood of Vancouver Island the face is very long and the nose is high and prominent, which changes the entire appearance.[1]

Being, like the Eskimo, essentially a maritime people, the arts and industries of the coast Indians which are connected with the sea are particularly well developed; but with a relatively warm and wet climate instead of an arctic environment, the line of evolution has been quite different. The

[1] Boas, in British Assoc. Advancement of Science, *Twelfth Report on the Northwestern Tribes of Canada*, 1898.

skin canoe gives place to the wooden "dug-out," which is hollowed from a single log, usually of cedar, and is found in all sizes from eight to forty feet or more in length, the larger canoes being thoroughly sea-worthy and capable of making long excursions along the coast.   Fish-hooks, spears, nets, and lines of great variety and efficiency have been devised, and among all these tribes the capture of salmon, halibut, and eulachon or candle-fish is the chief employment of the men.   Agriculture is practically unknown, but vegetable food is represented by berries and roots, which are gathered by the women and are found in great abundance on the luxuriant slopes of the main-land and the adjacent islands.

With the excessive rain-fall of the region some permanent and effective type of dwelling became a necessity, and the result is a huge, square type of house built of roughhewn cedar planks and roofed in with bark.   Houses of this character, forty and fifty feet square, are not uncommon, and some of the earlier explorers report them of much greater size.   The interiors are divided into rooms or compartments, each for a separate family.

A noticeable feature of these coast villages is the totem poles, which are carved from the trunks of trees and are really heraldic columns.   They are placed in front of the houses of chiefs, and record in sculpture the tradition of the owner's family or clan.   Among the southern tribes of the group totemic designs of a similar nature are painted on the sides and roofs of the houses.

From the point of view of culture, however, the most important characteristic of these Indians is their system of social organization, which is close and strictly guarded. In the north the tribes are divided into clans, each of which has its animal totem, and the clan relationship is traced through the mother.[1] The clans are further gathered into phratries, or groups, which are probably subdivisions of what were formerly single clans, and within these phratries marriage is forbidden. The system is most rigid in the northern tribes, but shows signs of weakening in the southern peoples. For instance, a new-born child whose father's clan has become weak in numbers may under certain circumstances and with appropriate ceremonial be entered as a member of the paternal clan when he would normally belong to that of his mother.

Among the Kwakiutl of Vancouver Island we find an interesting case of a people originally organized on a system reckoning descent through the father, who have come under the influence of maternal institutions, and adopted them in a way directly contrary to what is classically considered the usual course of development of the family and society.[2] This state of things, if correctly interpreted, has a most important bearing on the general

[1] See below, chap. xiii.
[2] Boas, *Social Organization of the Kwakiutl Indians*, 334.

theory of the evolution of the family.   In this tribe,
clan and family crests, names, and privileges are an
inheritance, and are held by a man either in his own
right, derived directly from his father, or in trust
for his children, and derived from his father-in-law
through his wife.   There are thus two sets of in-
heritances existing side by side, and the complexity
of the social organization in a tribe diminishing in
numbers like the Kwakiutl is too baffling to unravel.

An economic development among these tribes
which is of great interest and to which insufficient
attention has been paid hitherto is the so-called
"potlatch." [1]   This is at first glance a ceremonial
giving away of property, and as such has been
misunderstood and actively combated by missionaries and government agents on the ground that
it pauperized the natives.   It is in reality an
elaborate and beneficial system of credit.   In any
undertaking the Indian calls upon his friends for
help in the shape of loans.   These are always repaid
with interest at a later date, and, owing to lack of
a system of writing, such payments or repayments
are always made publicly, to give security to the
transaction.   This public negotiation, which is conducted with elaborate ceremonial and feasting, is the
potlatch.   The unit of value is the blanket, valued
at fifty cents, and as the amount of property owned
in every tribe greatly exceeds the number of blankets
actually in existence there, a set of economic con-

[1] Boas, *Social Organization of the Kwakiutl Indians*, 341.

ditions based on credit has grown up which is quite analogous to those present in any civilized community. The Indian of this region has as his main object in life the acquisition of property, and consequent social position for himself and his children. This involves the prompt payment of debts and the amassing of wealth, and the result of his efforts is the system just outlined. As an example of the independent growth of an elaborate financial system in a rude community, it stands almost, if not quite, unparalleled.

Strict social orders of chiefs, common people, and slaves also exist among these tribes, though in late years slavery has largely disappeared under the influence of whites. Wealth is the great means of attaining rank, and this is the explanation of the passion with which the northwest native seeks to obtain property.

The religion of these peoples is animistic and closely tied up with their totemic beliefs. Any individual may, if fortunate, obtain by proper fasting and training a supernatural helper, who will be one of the innumerable spirits supposed to exist in the world. By the aid of this helper the individual becomes a successful hunter or warrior or craftsman or seer, and the best shaman or medicine-man is the one who has the most powerful spirit at his command. This system of obtaining supernatural aid is more fully developed in the interior than on the coast, and, as will be brought out later, is a fundamental characteristic of Indian religious beliefs and cults.

Among the Kwakiutl, the clans are believed to have been founded by ancestors who had certain relations with supernatural beings and obtained from them the crests, names, dances, and songs. These are the privileges which are handed down from generation to generation and are jealously guarded as a family's most precious possession. Every year the spirits are supposed to visit the people and animate them, and it is during the times of their visits that the elaborate ceremonials which have often been described are conducted. It is impossible to disentangle the social and religious features of these systems, and the close relationship between the two is seen nowhere more clearly than in these tribes of the coast.

The chief figure in the mythology[1] of the region is the raven, who is the great benefactor of man. It is he who procures fire, daylight, and fresh water, regulates the phenomena of nature, and teaches men the arts. He is also a trickster, after the manner of the culture heroes of all American tribes. In certain places the mink assumes the leading rôle; and on the coast of Washington the same adventures that are told of the raven farther north are assigned to the bluejay.

Another distinctive feature of the culture of the northwest coast is the art. It is peculiar in

[1] Boas, *Indianische Sagen*, etc.

that the process of conventionalization of decorative patterns has not led, except in the case of Tlingit basketry,[1] to geometric designs, but to curiously conventionalized animal motives. The well-known totem poles and the carving and painting of house-posts, boxes, dishes, spoons, and implements of all sorts are examples of the process. The aim seems to be to portray as much of the pattern animal as possible; and in the adaptation of the design to surfaces of all shapes there has arisen a mode of conventional dissection and elimination of parts which is unique among primitive peoples.[2]

From Vancouver Island south to the Columbia River is a group of tribes of which the Nootka of the Wakashan family and numerous Salishan peoples about Puget Sound are the most conspicuous. They form a sort of transition in type between people of the north Pacific coast and the tribes of California, and do not demand extended description. The important factors to note are the rapid breaking-up of the close clan organization of society, the disappearance of the peculiar art mentioned above, the further development of certain industries, notably whaling, and the modification of the religious ceremonials and mythology by southern influence.

[1] Emmons, " Basketry of the Tlingit " (Am. Mus. Nat. Hist., *Memoirs*, III., 263).

[2] Boas, " Decorative Art of the Indians of the North Pacific Coast " (Am. Mus. Nat. Hist., *Bulletins*, IX.).

CHAPTER VIII

INDIANS OF THE NORTHERN INTERIOR AND OF THE LOWER PACIFIC COAST

(1800–1900)

PASSING up the Yukon River in Alaska, or the Mackenzie in British Columbia, or crossing the Coast Range in British Columbia, the widely distributed Athapascan family is encountered. This stock is often referred to as Tinné or Dènè, which is their own name for themselves wherever found, and signifies, as usual, "men" or "people." On the north the Athapascans come into contact with the Eskimo, on the south and east with the Algonquian tribes, and on the west with the Pacific peoples. Extensions of the stock south and west are numerous, small tribes who speak unmistakable Athapascan dialects appearing in Washington, Oregon, and California; while the important Navajo and Apache in New Mexico and Arizona form a branch of the family even more important numerically than that of British America.

The tribes which stretch across the north of the continent from the Coast Range to Hudson Bay occupy a bleak and barren territory and have never advanced far on the road to civilization. They are also cut up into a large number of tribes and bands, which speak mutually unintelligible dialects, but their manner of life as well as their physical features remain fairly uniform. The most important tribes of the northern branch are the Kutchin, Nahane, Slave, Taculli or Carriers, Chilcotin, Yellow Knives, Hare, Dogrib, Chippewyan, and Sarcee. On the Pacific slope various small tribes in southern Oregon and the Hupa of California may be noted, while the Navajo and Apache, already mentioned, represent the southern extension of the stock.

The same general culture stretches south from the northern Athapascan territory over the high plateaus between the Rockies and the Coast Range, through interior British Columbia, where it includes several inland Salishan peoples, notably the Shuswap and Thompson. Still farther south the Kootenay appear; and the important Shahaptian family, of which the Nez Percé and the Yakima are probably the best-known tribes, occupying a large part of eastern Washington, Idaho, and Oregon, must also be included. The Shahaptian stock is in intimate relation on the south with the great Shoshonean people. This latter family has an extensive distribution over Oregon, Idaho, Nevada, Utah, Colorado, southern California, New Mexico, and Texas. The northern Shoshone must be regarded as belonging to the plateau type of British Columbia

and the Shahaptian area. In all its branches the
Shoshonean family exhibits transitions to or mixt-
ures with surrounding culture. Its most important
tribes are the Ute, Shoshone, and Comanche, with
their constituent bands.

The distinguishing features of the culture of the
area we are discussing are the following: extreme loose-
ness of social organization, which stands in sharpest
contrast with the close systems of the coast; lack
of elaborate ceremonials; a complete change in the
character of the art; and possibly, also, the development of a mythology which, while not very different from that of the tribes to the east, bears
little resemblance to that of the northwest coast,
except in places where intimate affiliation has modified the normal type.

In general the clan system disappears entirely on
the plateaus, and even tribal organization can hardly
be said to exist. Independent local bands, under
leadership determined by circumstances or individual capacity, are the rule. These bands would
often affiliate for purposes of war or other ends, and
since common dialects and customs would determine the lines of the unions, tribal limits would tend
to appear. Local interests, however, often proved
stronger than tribal bonds, as was shown clearly
in the dealings with the whites during the settlement of Oregon and later. The Nez Percé war of
1876 is a good example, when a few bands under
Joseph conducted an active campaign, while the

majority of the tribe held entirely aloof or even sympathized with the United States, yet were not regarded as in any sense renegade to tribal obligations.

Little is known of the social organization of the northern Athapascans, but there is probably no clan system in operation, except in the case of the Carriers and possibly a few other tribes, where its nature pretty definitely proves its derivation from the Indians of the coast.[1] In general the two units are the immediate family and the local village group, but the latter is often unstable in character.

· The complex and elaborate religious ceremonials of the coast tribes are replaced by comparatively simple shamanistic practices. Prayers and observances are all directed towards mysterious, spiritual powers which are believed to pervade every phase of nature. The main object of every boy or girl is to obtain one of these spirits as his supernatural helper, who will then remain his guardian through life and to whom is given the credit for any success he may achieve. To acquire one of these guardian spirits is the object of the puberty ceremonials, which are particularly well developed in this group. As puberty approaches, the boy goes away by himself to an isolated spot, the peak of a mountain or a desert place, and there passes days or weeks in fasting and violent physical exercise

[1] Farrand, "The Chilcotin," in British Assoc. Advancement of Science, *Twelfth Report on the Northwestern Tribes of Canada*, 18.

combined with certain fixed symbolic rites.   During
the exhaustion thus produced, or in answer to the
nervous expectancy under which he lives, vivid
dreams or hallucinatory waking visions appear, and
in these is revealed to him the being who will act
as his helper n the future.

In order to become a recognized shaman of the
professional class, a much longer period of "training" is necessary.   Sometimes years are spent in the
acquisition of the necessary wisdom and powers.[1]
These customs will be noticed again in the general
discussion of Indian religious beliefs, but should
be emphasized here as forming the central interest
in the life of the people of this region.   In certain
of the tribes, as the Kootenay,[2] an annual ceremonial
is held which seems to be a sort of worship of the
sun, and connected with the idea of the possible
return of the dead from the other world.

The art of the plateaus is characterized by the
absence of the plastic forms which are so striking
on the coast.   Among many of these interior tribes
carving is practically unknown.   Decoration, therefore, consists largely in painted or woven designs,
which were undoubtedly originally attempts at
pictorial representations, but which have become,
through difficulties of execution, conventional in

[1] Teit, "The Thompson Indians of British Columbia" (Am.
Mus. Nat. Hist., *Memoirs*, II., 254 ff.).
[2] Cf. Chamberlain, in British Assoc. Advancement of Science,
Eighth Report on Northwestern Tribes of Canada.

form, but still, among most tribes, strictly symbolic. This characteristic is shown most clearly in the basketry[1] and in the painting of raw-hide receptacles of various kinds.

The mythology almost always refers to the deeds of a "transformer," or "transformers," who visited the world when it was in an incomplete state and straightened things out. He rid the country of monsters which infested it, changed and fixed the landmarks, taught the people the arts, and conferred upon them many benefits. After his work was done he disappeared, but is expected to return again when his people have most need of him.

This "transformer" is usually personified not as a venerable person, but as a coyote or one of the other animals, or some purely mythological being; he tricks and is tricked, indulges in the loosest amours, and is often vain, boastful, and petty in character; but is nevertheless the great benefactor and hero of the people.[2]

Of the industrial life of these tribes it is difficult to speak in general terms. They are all by necessity hunting and fishing peoples, but the contrast between the forests of the north and the arid region of the southern plateaus produces marked differences in the arts.

[1] Farrand, "Basketry Designs of the Salish Indians" (Am. Mus. Nat. Hist., *Memoirs*, II., pt. v.).
[2] Boas, in introduction to Teit, *Traditions of the Thompson Indians*.

The northern Athapascans are among the most primitive of all American stocks. They make a rude pottery and weave the hair of the mountain goat. Agriculture is unknown, and their livelihood is precarious and difficult. The advent of the Hudson Bay Company has affected the life of this group to a great extent, and much of their native manufacture has now given place to articles obtained from the posts in return for furs.

The Salishan tribes of British Columbia are somewhat more advanced. The former houses of these Indians were underground lodges covered in with roofs of beams, mats, and dirt. The excavation was three or four feet deep and eighteen to thirty feet in diameter; and from the edges four beams were inclined towards the centre, supported by posts and covered by cross-poles, woven mats, brush, and dirt. A hole was left at the apex, which served as the door and in which a ladder stood. The larger houses would be occupied by several families. These underground lodges were used only in winter, and in summer the people lived in tents of bark or mats woven of rushes. The household utensils were usually of basketry or bark.[1] Of late years these Indians, who are much in contact with whites, have given up most of their old industries, live in log huts, and have adopted the clothing and utensils of civilization.

[1] Teit, " The Thompson Indians of British Columbia" (Am. Mus. Nat. Hist., *Memoirs*, II., 192 ff.).

The Shahaptian and Shoshonean tribes of the more southerly plateaus were primarily hunting peoples, but the attraction of the salmon fisheries of the Columbia River seems to have very distinctly modified their habits of life. In general their existence was much like that of the Salishan tribes just mentioned, till the annual migration to the fisheries brought them into contact with Indians pushing up from the coast, and many customs were acquired in that way. For example, the communal houses of the Chinook were found among the Nez Percé when first seen by Lewis and Clark. The horse had also reached this group at the time of the explorers' visit, and the revolution which that acquisition would bring about is easy to imagine.

As has been pointed out, each group of these peoples has been influenced by foreign contact: the Athapascan by the Eskimo and north coast Indians; the Salishan by the coast tribes extending up the Fraser River; and the Shahaptian and Shoshonean by the lower Columbia peoples, as well as by the plains Indians on the east. There is no part of the continent where the migration of culture along natural paths of communication can be better studied than here, where the inhabitants are bordered by two diametrically opposed types, that of the coast and that of the plains.

Physically these stocks are strongly differentiated from the coast types and not so strongly from those of the plains. In stature the inland people are tall,

well built, and muscular. The chief facial feature
to be noted is the nose, which becomes strongly
marked, particularly among the Shahaptian and
Shoshonean tribes. The cheek-bones are wide and
prominent, the lips are thick, and the lower part of
the face is broad and heavy. These features appear at their best and most typically in the Indians
of the great plains, though in that region they lack
the coarseness which is the chief characteristic of
the Shoshonean and other tribes of the southern
plateaus.

From their homes on the plateaus the Shahaptian
and other peoples controlled the upper reaches of the
Columbia and its tributaries; and, led by the de-
sirability of salmon as an article of diet, they gradually pushed down that stream, until their extensions were checked by a people from the coast
of sharply different language and culture, the
Chinook.[1] The limiting line between these two
groups was at the falls of the Columbia in the neighborhood of the present city of The Dalles. On
account of their intimate relations with the early
traders on the lower Columbia, the Chinook, though
now nearly extinct, played a most important rôle
in the early settlement and development of Oregon.
There were two well-marked divisions of the stock,
the upper and the lower; the former living in the
interior, but along the banks of the Columbia;
while the latter had their seat near the mouth of

[1] Boas, *Chinook Texts.*

that river, and extended but a short distance north and south on either side of its entrance to the sea.

The general culture of the Chinook was much like that of the coast tribes farther north, especially in those phases which concerned their industrial life. The clan organization had, however, disappeared, and the mythology and religion began to take on new elements which showed the influence of Californian neighbors. The physical type is still the northern, with the heavy, broad face and short, thick-set body. The prevalent custom of deforming the head of infants by fronto-occipital pressure was practised universally by the Chinook, and they with their neighbors of Puget Sound may be regarded as the stronghold of the practice. It was in vogue as far south as the Yakonan family of tribes along the Óregon coast, where an intrusion of Athapascan stock occurs and the custom disappears.

The most important legacy of the coast Chinook is the Chinook jargon or trade language, which sprang up as a medium of intercourse between the whites and Indians and is a compound of Chinook words with English, French, and Spanish, all modified to meet the needs of pronunciation of the different peoples using it. It has now spread north as far as Alaska, south into California, eastward to the peoples beyond the Coast Range, and along natural routes of communication, such as the Columbia, the Fraser, etc., to points far inland.

The culture of the upper branch of the Chinook was practically that of their cousins of the coast, except where the absence of the sea produced a modification in their industrial life. Living in close contact, too, with the tribes of the plateaus, interchange of cultural elements took place between the two groups, so that, as already indicated, certain Chinook customs can be found among the Shahaptian tribes, and vice versa.

Early in the nineteenth century the Klikitat tribe of the Shahaptian pushed across the Coast Range and up the Willamette Valley, driving previous occupants ahead of them; but they were unable to hold the territory and after a few years retired to their former seat north of the Columbia River. The Willamette Valley just mentioned is one of the most fertile and desirable in the northwest and was naturally an objective point of early white emigration. It appears to have been occupied by a number of tribes of the Kalapooian family who were not particularly warlike or vigorous, and who yielded to the pressure of the settlers even though they had previously been able to retain their frontiers against the attacks of neighboring Indians.

Lying south and east of the Willamette Valley, with their centre about Klamath Lake, in southern Oregon, were two vigorous and warlike tribes, the Klamath and the Modoc, the latter of whom became widely known through the insurrection of 1869. The two tribes are closely related, forming the Lutuamian linguistic family, and are also possibly akin to the Shahaptian. They led a free hunting and fishing life and were the terror of the less vigorous tribes to the south and west. The Modoc, who formed the southern extension of the family, made annual raids into northern California for the capture of slaves, whom they carried to The Dalles and traded with the other tribes who congregated at that point. They had no clan organization and led a life similar to that of their Shahaptian neighbors.

Peculiar developments of the Klamath were their characteristic earth-covered lodges and the gathering of water-lily seeds for food. These plants grow in great abundance in Klamath Lake and vicinity, and seem to have been a decided factor in determining the habitat of this group of Indians.[1]

South of the Chinook and west of the Kalapooian tribes there ranged along the sea-coast of Oregon a series of small and relatively unimportant linguistic stocks, of which the Yakonan[2] about Yaquina Bay may be regarded as a type. Though living on and near the coast, they seem to have depended more upon the rivers and land than upon the sea for their food supply. The Yakonan tribes exhibit the generally coarse facial formation and undersized stature of the northern coast peoples, and are

---

[1] Gatschet, *The Klamath Indians.*
[2] Farrand, " The Alsea Indians of Oregon " (*American Anthropologist*, N. S., III., 239).

interesting as marking the southern limit of the practice of head deformation in that region. South of them tattooing makes its appearance, but it is not known among the tribes of Yakonan stock.

The Yakonan family marks the southern extension of the typical northwest coast culture and begins to show the influence of Californian contact. The character of the mythology shows decided changes: the culture hero or "transformer" no longer plays the part exhibited by the raven and bluejay of the north. Their religious conceptions are those most common to the Indian wherever found—i. e., wide-spread animism, with the institution of shamans, or medicine-men, well developed. The individual could acquire the supernatural helper or guardian in the usual way by "training" and fasting, but there is no evidence that it was hereditary in either line.

The usual social orders of nobility or chiefs, common people, and slaves prevailed; and it was possible for a man of common origin to raise himself to the rank of chief by reason of extraordinary wisdom, power, or wealth. The privileges of rank were, however, as a rule, guarded jealously. In matters of inheritance no preference was shown for either the male or female line, a child being regarded as related equally to both father's and mother's family.

In northern California and southern Oregon occurs one of the puzzling intrusions of the Athapascan family; indeed, the present state of California is characterized by a hodge - podge of linguistic stocks, which a glance at the linguistic map will make evident.   The physical type of California, if it be proper to speak of such, seems to be something intermediate between the coarse coast features and the finer facial make - up of the southwest.   The extreme southern part of the state is occupied by Shoshonean and Yuman tribes, the former belonging to the culture of the western plateau and the latter to the southwestern peoples in general.

Recent researches[1] show that the twenty - one linguistic families of California (exclusive of Yuman) fall into three groups, on a basis of grammatical affinities, and that this classification is corroborated to a certain extent by differences of culture in the groups in question.

The northwestern group of five small stocks differs from the others in the character of its art, the extensive use of canoes, the importance of salmon as an article of food, the development of ideas of property and their influence on social conditions, and the character of ceremonials, myths, and religious conceptions.

The central group is quite sharply marked off from the northwestern in point of culture; and the character and quest of the food supply must be regarded as the determinant factor.   The tribes of

[1] Dixon and Kroeber, "The Native Languages of California" (*American Anthropologist*, N. S., V., 1 ff.).

this group are universally dependent upon the acorn for food, and in its use and treatment have lost many of the characteristics which distinguish their neighbors. The canoe is noticeable for its absence, the myths differ sharply from those of the other groups, and we find appearing again certain ceremonials and secret societies the origin of which is puzzling.

The main tribe of this group, the Maidu, practises an annual ceremony known as the "burning," which is quite unique in its special development and of great interest in the light it throws on religious beliefs and conceptions.[1] At a stated time, with much preliminary form and ritual, the surviving relatives burn property of all sorts for the benefit of the dead, the idea being that the articles so destroyed pass to the spirit world and are there made use of by the spirits of the departed. This custom is kept up usually for a period of five years after the death of any individual, and then ceases, except in special cases where the deceased may have been a man of great prominence or his survivors persons of unusual piety.

Of the southwestern Californian group so little is known that nothing definite can be said regarding it. There is, however, a remarkable development of the canoe, a return to dependence on fish for food, and possibly a special type of art, particularly in carving.

[1] Dixon, *MSS. Notes*, in library of Am. Mus. Nat. Hist.

CHAPTER IX

THE INDIANS OF THE GREAT PLAINS
(1700–1900)

THE striking inequality in the geographical distribution of Indian stocks becomes most apparent in passing from the Pacific coast territory to the great basin of the continent. Practically five-sixths of all the linguistic families of North America are found along the western slope. The immense territory lying east of the Pacific mountain ranges is peopled by a few large, strong stocks, broken into many tribes and dialects, it is true, but with affiliations within the families that are usually more or less apparent. Of these stocks the most important are the Algonquian, Athapascan, Iroquoian, Muskhogean, Shoshonean, Siouan, and a few others of less moment and extent.

Since the physical features of their habitats produced conditions of climate and organic life totally different from those of the Pacific slope, differentiations of culture must appear equally marked. The first area which presents a possible unit of homogeneous aboriginal culture is the region of the great plains. To its inhabitants various stocks contributed, but chiefly the Siouan, Caddoan or Pawnee, Algonquian, and Kiowan in the order named. It would be impossible to take up the tribes of this area in detail, and the Sioux may serve as a type.

In the history of the United States the Sioux have been more noticeable than any other aborigines, with the exception of the Algonquian and Iroquoian tribes. They are often regarded, too, as the typical native Americans, physically strong and active, hunters and warriors by nature and necessity, shifting from place to place, but always free, always dominant, always significant. In comparison with the Indians of the Pacific coast their facial features are more strongly marked, the nose and the lower jaw being particularly prominent and heavy. The heads are, as a rule, mesocephalic and are not artificially deformed. The skin is dark, with a faint tinge of reddish. With the pressure of civilization and the relatively sedentary life which the Sioux have been forced to adopt of late years, their bodily vigor is not so striking as it once was; but they still remain, with their neighbors of the plains, a fine physical type of the American Indian.

In the distribution of the Siouan family, as a glance at the map will show, their main seat at the advent of the whites was the region west of the Mississippi, from the Saskatchewan in the north to the Arkansas in the south, though isolated offshoots appear in Virginia and on the Gulf of Mexico. Lin-

guistic evidence and to a certain extent native
tradition (Mandan) point to an Appalachian origin
for the group, and would indicate the eastern
slopes of that range as their earlier home. From
here they pushed westward, overrunning the prairies
and plains until brought to a halt by pressure from
the western stocks; while a back flow was prevented by the barrier offered by the Algonquian
tribes in their rear.

The one factor which has overshadowed all others
in its influence on the Sioux habitat, institutions,
art, and beliefs was the buffalo. Probably the
pursuit of the bison led westward the eastern tribes,
and notably the Sioux, and dispersed them over
the plains. The pre-eminent part which the buffalo
played in the nutrition and industrial life of these
peoples accounts, too, for their relatively slight
development of agriculture. With the arrival of
the horse, which was probably acquired by the
prairie tribes towards the end of the eighteenth
century,[1] the successful pursuit of the bison herds
was greatly aided; and this gave the final touch to
their mode of life.

There is good evidence that the dog had been
domesticated by the Sioux long before the appearance of the horse, and was used for food, draught,
and ceremonial sacrifice.[2] The chief industries of
the Sioux and their neighbors were naturally those

---

[1] McGee, in Bureau of Ethnology, *Fifteenth Annual Report*,
173.   [2] Zu Wied, *Travels*, etc.

of hunting and war. Weapons and implements
were of stone, wood, bone, horn, and antler. The
tomahawk, club, flint knife, and bow and arrow
were the usual weapons, but short spears were also
fairly common. Household utensils were few and
crude. Rude pottery and basketry were made,
but wood and skins furnished the raw material for
domestic service.

In addition to the food supply obtained by hunting, all the tribes of the plains made use of nuts,'
berries, roots, and other plants which were to be
found in a wild state, but which were also cultivated
after a fashion, whenever the residence was stable
enough to permit it. Agriculture did not, however,
flourish to any great extent except among the
Mandan.

The houses of the Sioux varied with the habitat
and the season. In the woodlands they built tent-
shaped lodges of saplings covered with brush, bark,
or skins. On the plains and prairies earth lodges
were constructed for winter, and tipis covered with
buffalo skins for the summer season. The tipi,
which is one of the typical forms of Indian dwellings,
is essentially a portable affair, and thus differs from
the wigwam of the east, which was fixed. It is
constructed of long poles tied together near the
smaller ends, with the bases spread out in a circle
ten or fifteen feet in diameter. It is then covered
with a skin or canvas wrapping, laced or pinned
together along the middle of the junction. The

upper part of this tent is left open to act as a smoke
vent and to create a draught for the fire, which is
built in the centre of the structure; the lower part
is left separated as a door and is covered with a
skin flap. The bottom of the entire covering is
fastened to the ground with pins or weighted with
stones. Among certain of the Siouan tribes these
tipis were elaborately decorated with symbolic
designs. The structure and local arrangement of
the lodges of the Siouan stock were generally determined in certain features by religious considerations and ritual as well as by the clan relationship
of the owners.[1]

The Mandan tribe of this family, who seem to
have developed along special lines, built rather an
elaborate structure, circular in outline and as much
as forty to sixty feet in diameter. The frame-work
was of stout posts and beams, the roof was conical,
and the whole covered in with mats, grass, and hard-
packed earth.[2] The interior was divided into triangular compartments, each of which was assigned
to a family and separated from the others by
partitions of decorated mats and skins. Villages
of such structures were surrounded by a stockade
of posts and were practically impregnable to the
methods of Indian warfare.

Essentially land‑dwellers, the Sioux and their

---

[1] Dorsey, " Siouan Cults " (Bureau of Ethnology, *Eleventh
Annual Report*).

[2] Catlin, *Letters and Notes*, II., 81.

neighbors made little use of canoes; but a form
of coracle constructed of skins by the Dakota women
was noticed at an early date by white visitors, and
together with certain vague linguistic suggestions
gave rise to the absurd theory that the Sioux were
of Welsh extraction,[1] an idea on a par with another
popular vagary that the Indians are the descendants of the lost tribes of Israel.[2]

The art of the Sioux was exhibited at its best
in the calendars and records which the men were
given to drawing and painting upon prepared buffalo skins, and also in the carving of the soft red
catlinite which was obtained in the Sioux territory
and widely used for pipes and especially for the
ceremonial calumets.   In these pipes symbolism was
developed to a high degree, but the significance was
greatest in the decoration of the stem, which was
often many feet in length, and descended from
father to son or was transferred to a successor with
much elaborate ceremonial.   The smoking of these
pipes was an indispensable part of any formal
function and particularly in any intertribal transaction.

Great care was also given by other plains tribes
to the decoration of the raw-hide "parfleches," or
packing-cases, and the study of the designs in use for
their embellishment has recently thrown much light
on certain problems connected with the develop-

[1] Catlin, *Letters and Notes*, II., App. A.
[2] Adair, *History of the American Indians*.

ment of primitive art.[1] Almost always symbolic, it has been found that these patterns and types of patterns are widely distributed, but that the interpretation differs, and differs sharply; and that while designs are readily adopted from foreign soil, the natives in all cases read a meaning into them.

The religious conceptions were based upon a belief in "Wakanda" or "Manitou"—or "mystery," as it is best translated—an all-pervading spiritual entity, differentiated in an indefinite number of individual forms, in the cult of which the various religious and shamanistic ceremonials developed. These ceremonials are particularly elaborate among Siouan tribes, and consisted of dancing and chanting, feasting and fasting, and in tests of physical endurance which sometimes reached degrees of bodily torture, as in the often - described "sun-dance," which have called forth ill - advised interference by the government authorities.

In the mythology of the group the sun is a prominent element, and in addition there are innumerable tales of mythical monsters, usually with animal or bird characteristics, and the atmosphere of the whole is tinged by the hunting and military habits of the tribes. The most distinctive of the ceremonials of the entire region is the sun-dance just mentioned. It is found under one name or

[1] Kroeber, "Decorative Symbolism of the Arapaho" (*American Anthropologist*, N. S., III., 308).

another among practically all of the stocks and tribes of the plains except the Comanche. It is an elaborate annual ceremonial in which the sun is invoked, but chiefly thanked for favors bestowed upon his devotees. It is participated in by practically all the adult members of the tribe, is managed by the recognized shamans or medicine-men, and the leading parts are taken by the secret societies of a military character which are found in nearly all the tribes. While it is thus a general tribal ceremony, it is always prepared and given by some individual in fulfilment of a vow.

A ceremonial lodge of saplings is erected, and on the centre pole a sacred bundle containing symbolic shamanistic charms is suspended. The dancers form a semicircle, and with their eyes fixed on the sacred bundle keep up a constant shrill whistling through eagle bones held in the teeth, accompanied by characteristic movements of the arms and bodies. The participants are naked and painted with symbolic designs, which are frequently changed during the ceremony. The dance lasts four days as a rule, and among certain tribes, notably the Mandan, the later stages were marked by the physical tortures noticed above. The flesh of the breast and shoulders was pierced by wooden skewers to which thongs were attached and upon which the dancer threw his weight until he tore himself loose. The dance is accompanied by singing and drumming, and throughout the performance there are many addresses, initiations, and other less formal functions of a purely social character.

The social organization of the Sioux[1] is characterized by kinship groups, with inheritance, as a rule, in the male line.   Traces of female descent are, however, met, and in the lodge the woman was to a certain extent autocratic.   Marriage was arranged by the parents, and polygamy was common where the man was capable of supporting more than one wife. Exogamy with respect to the clan was strictly enforced, but marriage within the tribe or between related tribes was encouraged.   There can be no doubt that the marriage relations between tribes of Siouan stock did much to strengthen the feeling of unity which marked certain confederations among them.

The regulations with regard to property were fairly complex.   The ownership of land was vested in the group which occupied it.   Food was shared in common, with certain privileges reserved for the individual who had procured it.   Lodges, dogs, weapons, etc., belonged to the individual, and strictly personal property was usually destroyed at the death of the owner.   It has been held by some that the purpose of this destruction was to avoid future disputes as to ownership;[2] but while this

---

[1] Dorsey, "Siouan Sociology" (Bureau of Ethnology, *Fifteenth Annual Report*).

[2] McGee, in Bureau of Ethnology, *Fifteenth Annual Report*, 178.

may have been a factor, there can be little doubt that the custom arose here, as in other regions, in the desire to provide for the deceased in the next world.

The government of the Siouan tribes, such as it was, consisted in a leadership of chiefs, who attained their position by personal prowess, and who, as is the rule among primitive peoples, were pre-eminent mainly in times of particular emergency. This chieftainship does not appear to have been hereditary except in so far as the requisite qualities might tend to appear in the same families. Elder men of recognized sagacity and experience also exercised great influence in times of peace, but were hardly on the same plane with the military leaders.

The main families of the great plains, other than the Siouan, were the Caddoan or Pawnee and the Kiowan. The former was scattered in groups from the Gulf of Mexico to what is now the state of North Dakota. The Pawnee tribes were probably of southern origin and migrated northward, coming into contact and struggle with the Siouan peoples as they advanced. Physically and culturally they are not very sharply differentiated from the Sioux except in a few phases. Like the Sioux, the Pawnees were of strong physique but with a somewhat finer cast of features. The lips were thinner and the lower part of the face more delicately chiselled.[1] They were divided into kinship groups, distinguished

---

[1] Brinton, *American Race*, 95.

by totems, and the inheritance was apparently in the male line.   The tribes of the stock were divided into bands, more or less independent, and chieftainship in the bands was much more developed than among the Sioux.   The office was hereditary in the male line, and the chief's power much more absolute than was usual among the Indians.

Agriculture was more commonly practised than among other peoples of the plains, and fields were regularly planted and cultivated by individual families: maize, pumpkins, and squashes were the leading products.   During the months of the year when the tribes occupied fixed residences they built a characteristic form of house, which is still known as the Pawnee type, though not entirely confined to that stock.   A circular frame-work of poles or logs was covered in by brush, bark, and earth, affording a thorough protection and a home permanent enough for their needs.   When on the move, as in the buffalo-hunt, they used lodges of skins arranged over a frame-work of poles.   Crude pottery of a rough type was manufactured by the women, and in general the domestic utensils were simple.

The Pawnee religious ceremonials, while of much the same general character as those in use among the Sioux, are more elaborate and occupy a far greater portion of the people's time and attention. The most distinguishing feature of the Pawnee religious rites was formerly the human sacrifices offered to the morning star on the occasion of the annual corn-planting, the victim being usually a captive girl from some hostile tribe. The custom persisted until very recently and was broken up with great difficulty.

The Kiowa roamed farther to the west and were always nomadic. They were close neighbors of the Shoshonean tribes, and they may prove to be linguistically affiliated with that stock, though the evidence is regarded as favoring their independence. The main physical distinction is a rather light skin color. They were always noted marauders, and seem to have lived mainly by hunting and by depredations on neighboring tribes. In their intercourse with the whites they were consistently hostile and unruly.

The Kiowa lodges were light tipis of skin which could be quickly struck and moved by means of horses, which they owned in great numbers. Their religion is very similar to that of the plains Indians already described, the sun-dance extending its sway over them as well as the others. The clan organization is not found among the Kiowa, but the tribe is divided into six bands, all well recognized and defined.

Among the plains people are several Algonquian and Shoshonean tribes who have adapted themselves to the region. In northern Montana and on the Canadian side of the boundary in the foot-hills of the Rockies live the Blackfoot, an Algonquian people, divided into two groups, the Blood and the Piegan, who have joined to themselves an Athapascan tribe of the north, the Sarcee, and formed a close confederation. Their culture is much the same as that of the Siouan tribes who border them on the south, but also contains certain elements which may be either a reminiscence of their former home in the east or the result of more recent contact with the Ojibwa and other Algonquian relatives.

The Arapaho and Cheyenne are also Algonquian tribes who became cut off from the bulk of their family in the early western migration and have become true representatives of the plains. They are chiefly distinguished by certain peculiar social developments, particularly among the Cheyenne.

On the southern plains the Comanche of Shoshonean lineage have for over a century been closely associated with the Kiowa, and being like them of a roving and turbulent disposition, formerly extended their depredations as far south as Mexico. Physically the Comanche retain something of the heavy-featured face of the true Shoshone and are in general of a rather low type of culture. They are singularly deficient, for a tribe of the plains, in religious ceremonials; and their social system is loose and disorganized, as might be expected from their plateau inheritance.

Several common features, not already discussed, are characteristic of these groups of the west. In most of them have sprung up societies or organizations of a military and religious character which are often secret, require formal initiation, and play a most important part particularly in the ceremonial life of the tribes. In many of them there are regular degrees through which a member passes after fulfilling the necessary requirements, in much the same way as obtains in similar orders among civilized peoples. It is quite possible that this institution and the rather elaborate religious ceremonials which have been spoken of may not be of indigenous growth but are a degenerate extension from Mexico and the southwest.

Another interesting achievement of the plains Indians is the so-called "sign language."[1] The unstable character of their residences and the frequency with which they came into contact with groups speaking unintelligible dialects made some common means of communication necessary, and the result was a combination of gesture and grimace of remarkable efficiency. It became developed to an extraordinary degree, and while doubtless in its origin it was largely descriptive, with the meaning evident in the sign, it became through generations of use conventional to such a degree that no one unacquainted with it could understand more than a fraction of the gestures current over the enormous territory in which it was used.

[1] Mallery, *Introduction to Study of Sign Language among North American Indians; Collection of Gesture Signs*, etc.

Notwithstanding the fact that the region occupied by these Indians of the plains had been visited as early as 1541 by De Soto and Coronado, but little was known of them until the early part of the nineteenth century. A certain amount of trade had been carried on with the southern tribes from the French settlements on the lower Mississippi, and the Sioux and other northern groups had been visited by French traders shortly after the discovery of that great waterway. It was not, however, until after the Louisiana Purchase that the whites entered the region in any numbers. Following that transaction the first to come were the fur - traders, and within a few years numerous posts were founded and regular routes of travel established to the mountains beyond the plains. The Indians were not averse to trade, and usually welcomed the traders because of the opportunity afforded to obtain hitherto unheard of luxuries. No great difficulties arose at first, though there were some losses, both of property and lives, through hostile bands, or because of rash or unjust acts on the part of the whites.

As the immigrants began to pour into and through the country matters became more serious. The opportunity thus offered to the Indians to revenge injuries, fancied or real, and to acquire great wealth without much danger to themselves, was often too tempting to be resisted by the hot - headed younger element, even when opposed by the sager counsels of the old men; and even the older Indians soon saw that the endless procession of on-coming whites foreboded no good for the future of their own race.

The different tribes varied much in the degree of hostility. The Pawnee, though much dreaded by the early traders,[1] were, as a tribe, never at war with the whites, and frequently furnished scouts in the various difficulties that arose with other Indians. In the south the Comanche were particularly notorious and a constant source of trouble and danger, both to immigrant trains and border settlements. The Sioux, the largest and most important of the plains tribes, were also the cause of some of the most serious of the Indian wars. Even as early as the War of 1812 they sided with the British against the Americans; but their worst outbreak was in 1862, when nearly one thousand settlers were killed in Minnesota. For the next six years there was almost constant war with the Sioux, Cheyenne, Kiowa, and other tribes of the region. The invasion of their country after the discovery of gold in the Black Hills again led to a serious outbreak in 1876–1877, during which the Custer massacre took place. The last serious outbreak, due to dissatisfaction at their treatment and the excitement aroused by the reported coming of an Indian messiah,[2] was in the winter of 1890–1891.

[1] Chittenden, *American Fur Trade*, 869.
[2] Mooney, " The Ghost-Dance Religion " (Bureau of Ethnology, *Fourteenth Annual Report*).

CHAPTER X

NORTHERN TRIBES OF THE EASTERN WOODLANDS

(1600–1900)

WITH a few unimportant exceptions, the tribes of the northeast were of one or other of two linguistic families, the Algonquian and the Iroquoian. The former occupied by far the greater territory, and in the history of the United States played decidedly the more important rôle. The Algonquian stock stretched from the Athapascan frontier in British America around the southern shore of Hudson Bay, included the interior of Labrador, and sweeping south covered the territory of the Great Lakes and all the eastern part of Canada and the eastern states as far south as Tennessee. Its most westerly extension is the Blackfoot tribe, which lies along the base of the Rocky Mountains at about the forty-ninth parallel, and is isolated by a body of Siouan peoples on its eastern border.

The most considerable break in the continuity of this Algonquian occupation was made by the strong and important Iroquoian tribes who surrounded

lakes Erie and Ontario, extended down the St.
Lawrence River on both banks to about the site
of Quebec, and occupied the greater part of New
York state and eastern Pennsylvania. A southern
branch of the Iroquois had its seat in eastern
Tennessee, northern Georgia, and parts of Virginia
and the Carolinas.

In the north the westward limit was reached by
the Blackfoot described above, who, in their adaptation to the environment of the plains, have assumed the culture which is typical of that area.
The general western limit of the Algonquians was
marked by the Siouan tribes at the Mississippi
Valley. The southern barrier was formed by the
Muskhogean family in the gulf states and a number
of small groups of different affinities along the
Atlantic seaboard in Virginia and the Carolinas.
In its most northerly extension the Algonquian
family is still checked by the Eskimo, who occupy
the shore of Labrador and formerly crossed the
strait of Belle Isle into Newfoundland. A small
and unimportant stock found in Newfoundland and
known as the Beothukan is now extinct; little is
known of them, but such linguistic evidence as can
be obtained points to their independence.

In the far north the Cree are the leading tribe
of the Algonquian family; while to the south and
west of them stretches the large Ojibwa division,
broken up into numerous bands, but centring in a
general way about the Great Lakes. In the east

the Micmacs of Nova Scotia and New Brunswick are prominent, while in New England a number of tribes of Algonquian lineage, such as the Abnaki, Mohegan, Massachusset, Narraganset, Pequot, Wampanoag, and others, occupied the territory to the exclusion of all other families. The Mohegan, of the lower Hudson, and the Delaware (Lenapé), of the Delaware Valley, brought the stock to the region of Chesapeake Bay. In Virginia were the Powhatan and related groups, and in Tennessee the Shawnee marked the southern limit of Algonquian occupation. A branch of the Shawnee is known to have pushed its way as far south as the Savannah River, but was later driven north, where it joined the Delaware.

The main tribes of the central Algonquians besides the Ojibwa, mentioned above, were the Sauk and Fox, two tribes originally independent but to-day practically one; the Illinois, Kickapoo, Menominee, Ottawa, Pottawotomi, and numerous others of less importance. The Cheyenne and Arapaho, two related tribes of the group, forced their way in the early migrations as far west as the Black Hills of South Dakota, and even into Wyoming and Colorado, where, closed in by Siouan and Shoshonean peoples, they have remained ever since.

Physically, the Algonquians are among the best of the aborigines, tall and strong, moderately dolichocephalic in head type, with the prominent nose and projecting malar bones which are regarded as characteristic of the American natives.

The mouth and lips are not as coarse as in the northwest, nor even on the plains, and the general facial effect is somewhat finer than in those regions. The skin is brown, with a very slight coppery tone.

The Algonquians were, as a rule, woodland people, with the culture, life, and craft which such residence brings about; but the wide differences in latitude between the seats of the northern and southern branches of the eastern Algonquians naturally brought about differences in their manner of life, Taking the largest tribe of the stock, the Ojibwa. as a type of the northern group, we find that they paid but little attention to agriculture and were essentially a hunting and fishing people, adding to the provision thus obtained such wild vegetable food as their country afforded. The wild rice was and is of such overwhelming importance to the Ojibwa that its annual harvest might be considered the central interest in their industrial life.[1] They also understood how to make sugar from the sap of the maple, and had knowledge of many edible fruits and seeds. The tendency to organize secret societies, which has been noticed in the stocks previously discussed, has found its expression among the Ojibwa in the Midé society,[2] a religious organization of elaborate rules and ritual which practically

---

[1] Jenks, " Wild-Rice Gatherers of the Upper Lakes " (Bureau of Ethnology, *Nineteenth Annual Report*).

[2] Hoffman, " The Midewiwen of the Ojibwa " (Bureau of Ethnology, *Seventh Annual Report*).

controls the religious life and ceremonials of the tribe.

As we range south among the Algonquian groups the most striking change is the increasing attention paid to agriculture. From New England down it was generally and quite extensively practised, maize, squash, and tobacco being the chief products.

The typical dwelling of the eastern Indians was a small hut built of saplings set firmly in the ground and bent together at the tops, forming a rounded frame. Through this were woven split poles and flexible branches, and the whole was covered in with leaves, reeds, bark, or brush. These were the so-called "wigwams," and in the northeastern section were usually set in groups; the villages thus formed were sometimes surrounded by a palisade of poles driven into the ground. Summer dwellings were often nothing more than carelessly made shelters of brush.

The Algonquians were organized on a totemic clan system, with descent, as a rule, in the female l ne. There was a chief of each clan, and commonly a tribal chief as well, who was chosen normally from one clan, in which the office was hereditary. This chief was of rather indefinite authority and did not interfere in matters concerning any one clan, but was appealed to on questions of general or inter-clan interests. In case of war a war-chief was selected on account of personal prowess, and took precedence over the permanent officers of the clans and tribes.

The religion of this group was, as usual, the belief in "manitou," or mystery, individualized in innumerable forms and brought into relation with man through various rites and ceremonies of shamanistic character. The general conceptions are best brought out in the mythologies of the group, which have to do with a great number of "manitous" of varying powers and character. There is always one—*e. g.*, Manibozho—who plays the leading rôle and is the benefactor and culture hero of the tribe. His exploits and adventures are related in great detail and form a cycle of myths about which the other stories cluster. It was in the early misconception of this character and his representatives in the different Algonquian tribes that the prevalent erroneous notion of the "Great Spirit" of the Indians had its origin.[1]

The Iroquoian tribes which break the continuity of the Algonquian domain form, in many ways, the most interesting group on the continent. In general culture they are not to be differentiated from the stocks around them, but in political development they stand unique. The main seat of the family was on the St. Lawrence River and in New York state. In the latter area the so-called Five Nations — the Mohawk, Onondaga, Oneida, Cayuga, and Seneca—formed a barrier to Algonquian

[1] See chap. xvi., below.

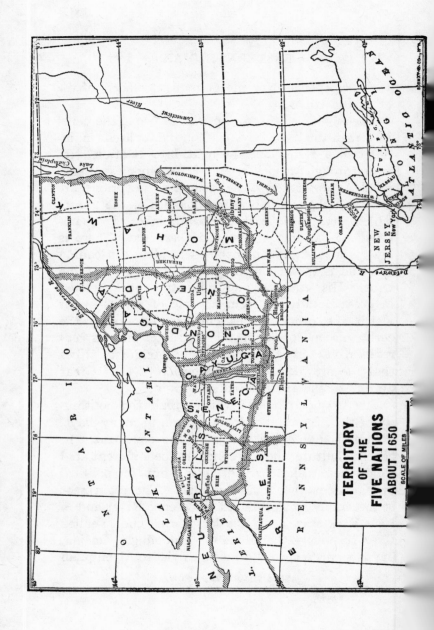

TERRITORY
OF THE
FIVE NATIONS
ABOUT 1650

SCALE OF MILES

movement and influence from the Hudson River to the lakes. West of these tribes the Wyandot, or Huron, and the Neutral Nation held the country between lakes Ontario and Huron; while south of Lake Erie lived the tribe from which that lake takes its name. In the valley of the Susquehanna and south to the Potomac were the Conestoga, or Susquehannock, while still farther south on the Roanoke River were the Tuscarora. On the Tennessee River lived the Cherokee, who are now pretty definitely proven to be of Iroquoian stock, but will be described independently.

The special achievement of the Iroquois was the organization, probably between 1400 and 1450, of the famous League of the Iroquois,[1] a confederation of the Five Nations just named, for purposes of defence and offence. The conception of the league is traditionally ascribed to a Hiawatha, who may or may not have been an historical personage, who, it is said, enlisted the support of a leading chief of the Onondaga; and acting in concert they succeeded in successfully carrying out the idea.[2] The salient features of the league were that it was a confederacy of the five tribes, each remaining independent in matters of local concern but delegating supreme authority in questions of general import to a council of sachems elected from the con-

---

[1] Morgan, *League of the Iroquois; Ancient Society; Houses and House Life*, etc.; Hale, *Iroquois Book of Rites;* Colden, *History of the Five Nations.*　　[2] Hale, *Iroquois Book of Rites*, 21.

stituent tribes.[1] The members of this council were
limited in number and were equal in rank and
authority. Fifty sachemships were founded and
named in perpetuity in certain clans of the several
tribes, and these tribes retained the right to fill
vacancies by election or to depose for cause. The
right to invest a sachem-elect with office was reserved by the general council. These sachems of
the confederacy were sachems also in their several
tribes, and with the "chiefs" or leading men of these
tribes formed the tribal council. This tribal council
had supreme authority over all matters pertaining
exclusively to the tribe.

In the council of the confederacy unanimity was
essential to every act; and since in that body the
sachems voted by tribes, each tribe had a veto
power over all the others. The general council
could be convened by the call of the council of any
tribe, but it had no power to convene itself. It
was open to orators of the people for the discussion of public questions, the decision resting solely
with the elected sachems. The confederacy had no
executive or official head, but for great military
operations two war-chiefs were appointed, who were
made equal in rank and authority.

Space will not permit a detailed discussion of the
various phases of the organization: it was a magnifi-
cent conception and splendidly carried out. The

[1] For the procedure and details, see Hale, *Iroquois Book of
Rites;* Morgan, *League of the Iroquois, Ancient Society.*

weak point seems to have been the lack of provision
for an executive, but this was largely compensated
for by the power of public opinion in compelling
obedience to decrees of the council. Whatever
its inherent weakness, the league was so successful
that for centuries it enjoyed complete supremacy
over its neighbors. It was, apparently, not intended to be limited to the five original tribes, for
overtures were made to the related Erie, Huron,
and other tribes to join the league. The only success was in the case of the Tuscarora, who in 1715
migrated from their southern home and joined the
league under certain restrictions, making the group
the Six Nations. An unimportant branch of the
family between Lake Ontario and Lake Huron was
also included at that time. The other divisions of
the stock were treated as enemies, and many of the
most savage campaigns of the league were waged
against the Erie and the Huron.

This extraordinary scheme of representative government was made possible by the social system
which had developed among the Iroquois, and
which is well expressed in their mode of communal
living. The tribes of the stock were organized on a
totemic clan basis, with clan inheritance in the
mother's line; exogamy with regard to the clan was
strictly observed. The dwellings of the Iroquois[1]
were regularly the famous "long houses," which were
from fifty to one hundred feet long and fifteen to

---

[1] Morgan, *Houses and House Life*, 64.

twenty feet wide. The house was built of a stout frame-work of upright poles set in the ground, with horizontal supports to strengthen them, and the roof was either triangular or rounded. The whole was covered in with bark shingles, and a second frame-work on the outside held the covering firm. The interior was divided into compartments, roughly six or eight feet square, ranging along each side of the house and opening on a common passageway down the centre, in which the fires of the occupants were built. Sleeping-bunks were arranged around the walls of each chamber.

Each of these long houses was inhabited by related families, which would mean that the mothers and children were as a rule of the same clan, while the fathers were of other and various clans. As a consequence, one clan, that of the women, would predominate in the house, and it thus became a factor of importance in the general organization. Further, the system completely altered the general status of women in the group, for over each house a matron presided whose authority was almost absolute in matters of domestic economy, and any undesirable male occupant could be summarily expelled by the female element. The women also had a voice in the councils of the clan and could make their influence felt even in the deliberations of the general council of the confederacy, although they were not permitted to address that body in person.

The clan,[1] which was the fundamental unit of the Iroquois system, had a definite organization and officers. The official head of the clan was the "sachem," who was strictly a peace officer, and the position when vacant was filled by election from the members of the clan, which usage, since maternal inheritance ruled, prevented a son from succeeding his father. There were also "chiefs" of the clan, the number depending upon the numbers of the clan and upon the fitness of the available candidates. The function of the chiefs was military, and distinct from that of the sachems. The clan had always the right to depose its sachems or chiefs for cause.

Other rights and privileges reserved by the clan were: obligations of help, defence, and redress of injuries of members; right of inheritance of the personal property of deceased members, which passed to maternal relatives, and therefore remained within the clan limits; the right to bestow names upon its members, certain names being confined to certain clans; the right to adopt strangers or captives, and thus to strengthen the group; the observance of special religious ceremonials; and, above all, the council of the clan, in which all adults, men and women, had a voice, and which adjusted all affairs affecting the clan as a group. The council elected and deposed sachems and chiefs, avenged or

[1] An excellent summary of the functions of the clan is contained in Morgan, *Ancient Society*, 62 et seq.

condoned murders of clansmen, regulated adoption, and passed on other tribal affairs.

The clans were organized into phratries, mutually exogamous groups of clans which had no strictly governmental functions, and appear chiefly in religious ceremonials and games.

The tribe,[1] which formed the next step in the political organization of the Iroquois, was, as always, distinguished by a name, a dialect, and territory. It further had the privilege of deposing a chief or sachem, a right which pertained primarily to the clan, but was also vested in the tribe as a precautionary measure. The tribal council was composed of the chiefs and sachems of the clans and held ultimate authority over the tribe. It was open to address by any member of the tribe, man or woman, but the decision with regard to any question remained solely with the official members.

Military operations could be undertaken by any individual or body of men, with or without the sanction of the tribe or the confederation; and as a matter of fact many of the most destructive campaigns of the Iroquois were carried on by war parties of small numerical strength. Theoretically, every tribe was at war with every outlying tribe (including the whites) with which there was not an express treaty of peace; and so long as a given raid did not violate treaty obligations it was viewed with favor by the rest of the tribe or confederation,

---

[1] Morgan, *Ancient Society*, 102 et seq.

although the perpetrators had no right to demand assistance or recognition.

The close interrelation of the confederacy with the social organization of the group gave it more than political significance. The essential unit is the clan, and the sachems of the general council were primarily clan representatives. The communal house life served to emphasize and bring into constant practical prominence the clan feature, and it seems to have been recognized even by the Iroquois themselves as the prototype of their league, since they called themselves "People of the Long House," a figurative reference to the narrow line of confederated bands stretching from the Hudson to Niagara.

The formation of the League of the Iroquois entirely changed the political aspect of affairs over a vast territory. The Iroquois tribes, who had been driven from their homes on the St. Lawrence and were being steadily beaten back by their Algonquian enemies, at once stood firm and began to assume the defensive. They harried the Indians to the north and the south until they were virtual masters of the territory from Hudson Bay to North Carolina, and east and west they pushed their conquests until their borders were free from danger. Their northwestern extension was checked by the powerful Ojibwa at the eastern end of Lake Superior; and their own kindred, the Cherokee, were able to stop their progress southward. The important rôle which they played in the early days of European colonization is a matter of history.

Although the Iroquois created the best-known confederation, they were far from the only Indian confederates. A similar system united the Aztec of Mexico when found by the Spaniards, and the same fundamental features were seen in the organization of many other Indian groups, and will be treated in a more general way in a subsequent chapter.[1]

[1] See below, chap. xiii.

CHAPTER XI

SOUTHERN TRIBES OF THE EASTERN WOOD-LANDS

(1600–1900)

CENTRING about the valley of the Delaware River and occupying southeastern New York, eastern Pennsylvania, and practically all of New Jersey, were the powerful Delaware or Lenapé. They formed one of the largest and strongest of Algonquian tribes and were able to withstand for many years the attacks of the Iroquois, who bordered them on the north and west. They were finally forced to give way, however, and, leaving their original home, took refuge in the valley of the Susquehanna and upper Ohio. With the settlement of Pennsylvania and New Jersey the Delaware naturally came into close contact with the whites, and it was with this tribe that Penn made his famous treaty in 1682. The connection between the Delaware and their kindred of the New England states was made by the Mohegan, who occupied the lower Hudson. Manhattan Island, their farthest southern haunt, was never anything more than a hunting-ground for Mohegan bands, the nearest known permanent villages being on the north side of the Harlem River.

The next powerful aggregation of Algonquian stock appears in Virginia and was generally known as the Powhatan confederacy. This organization controlled nearly all of tide-water Virginia, and included as its chief members the Powhatan, Pamunkey, Chickahominy, and Potomac tribes. Its founder and leader was Wahunsonacook, or Powhatan, as he was usually called from the name of his tribe. Upon his death in 1618 his successor, Opechancanough, organized a campaign of extermination against the whites, and brought on a conflict which lasted with intermissions for about thirty years and resulted most disastrously for the Indians—the confederacy was completely broken up and some of the constituent tribes practically annihilated. Curiously enough, the Pamunkey still survive as a tribe and retain their organization, though nearly if not quite all the members are mixed bloods.[1] The information regarding these Indians of Virginia is not very complete, but they probably did not differ very decidedly in habits from their Algonquian relatives farther north. They were agricultural like their neighbors, and were organized on a clan system with inheritance in the female line. They seem to have developed special and elaborate religious ceremonials, and it is interesting to note that they used the wooden dug-out and not the bark canoe.

[1] Pollard, *The Pamunkey Indians of Virginia.*

Another group of important Algonquian peoples were the Shawnee, of Kentucky and Tennessee, and the Illinois group north of the Ohio. The Shawnee, or Shawano, were first described as occupying territory in South Carolina, but appear later in the valley of the Cumberland, and it is with that region that their name is chiefly connected. They were organized on a clan basis, with maternal inheritance, and also recognized four divisions, the character of which is not clear, though certain of them had hereditary privileges, such as the right of succession to the offices of shaman or priest. Industrially, the Shawnee are chiefly remarkable for their manufacture (from saline springs) of salt, which they used extensively for barter with surrounding tribes. The Shawnee were always a roving and warlike tribe and seem to have been higher than many of their neighbors in point of intelligence. They are now for the most part incorporated with the Cherokee Nation. The leading figure in Shawnee history is their great chief, warrior, and organizer, Tecumseh, whose part in the Indian outbreaks of 1811 and the War of 1812 is well known.

The Illinois formed a loose confederacy and were prominent in the early struggles between the French and English, and later, after the close of the Revolution, caused much trouble to the United States before they were subdued.

A characteristic of this great family of Indians was their skill in picture-writing. While by no means so far advanced as the systems in use in Mexico and Central America, the Algonquian pictography had reached a symbolic stage; and the records of the Ojibwa and Delaware on birch bark and wood are most valuable as exhibiting the process of development from picture to alphabetic writing.[1]

Returning to the mountains of the Carolinas, Tennessee, northern Georgia, and Alabama, we encounter another great branch of the Iroquoian family in the powerful tribe of the Cherokee. Their linguistic relationship with the Iroquois of New York was not very close, and they were not on friendly terms with their cousins of the league and hedged them in on the south. From 1540, when they first came into notice, until 1838, when they were removed to Indian Territory, the Cherokee were always a conspicuous element in the history of North America. They were probably the largest single tribe in the eastern United States, and from the ethnological point of view are interesting chiefly from the rapidity and success with which they have adopted the life and government of civilized nations. In 1820 they even went so far as formally to organize themselves with a definite constitution, under the name of the Cherokee Nation; but various troubles with the government of Georgia led to their removal, and since that time their tribal indepen-

[1] Hoffman, *The Beginnings of Writing;* Mallery, " Picture Writing of the American Indians" (Bureau of Ethnology, *Tenth Annual Report*).

dence and government, though kept up in form, seem to be gradually losing ground. When visited by De Soto they were living in large and permanent villages of log houses and practised agriculture extensively.[1]

From the Cherokee frontier to the gulf, and between the Atlantic and the Mississippi, the country was occupied by the Muskhogean or Maskoki family, of which the greater portion was included in the Creek confederacy, and as such divided honors with the Cherokee in early importance. The leading tribes of the stock were the Apalache, Chickasaw, Choctaw, Creek or Maskoki, and Seminole. Of these the Choctaw held the western frontier, on the Mississippi; the Chickasaw and Apalache the central region, in the present state of Alabama; while the Creek and Seminole occupied the eastern border, chiefly in the states of Georgia and Florida. The early writers comment on the striking diversity in physical type offered by the different branches of the family: the Creek were tall and slender, while the Chickasaw, their near relatives and neighbors, were short, stocky, and heavily built. There seems also to have been a considerable difference in customs between the eastern and the western members of the stock.

---

[1] Cf. Royce, "The Cherokee Nation of Indians" (Bureau of Ethnology, *Fifth Annual Report*); Mooney, "Myths of the Cherokee" (Bureau of Ethnology, *Nineteenth Annual Report*); Adair, *History of the American Indians*.

The dominant tribe was unquestionably the Creek, and we may regard them as the type of the stock for purposes of description.[1] They were organized on a clan system, with descent in the female line, but had a remarkably large number of clans, twenty being still in existence and a number of others remembered by the people. Several of these clans with their constituent families united to form a village, where they lived under one chief, or "miko"; and, being independent, such a community in reality formed a tribe by itself. The miko was elected for life from a certain clan, and was preferably the next of kin, on the maternal side, of the miko just deceased. If the miko became incapacitated from age or illness he chose a coadjutor, who was subject to the approval of the village council.

This council, composed of the leading men of the group, exercised great power, but mainly by persuasion or moral influence, for the lack of an executive is typical of Indian government everywhere and has already been noted in the case of the Iroquois. At the same time insubordination was infrequent, possibly because of the conservatism of the council. It seems that among the Creek every man felt himself more bound by the action of his own particular clan than by that of his village or tribe, a state of things which emphasizes the importance of the kinship group as the fundamental factor in the political organization of these Indians of the east.

[1] Cf. Gatschet, *Migration Legend of the Creek Indians.*

The position of the Creek among hostile and powerful neighbors naturally fostered a warlike spirit and brought into prominence and favor the warrior class. As an additional incentive a series of war titles had been instituted, and the gaining of these by prowess in the field became the over-whelming passion of the youthful "brave." To become a warrior, every young man had to pass through a period of severe training and initiation which lasted from four to eight months; and upon its completion he was eligible for service in the field and possible advancement to the higher titles. Of these degrees there were three, "leader," "upper leader," and "great warrior," all granted by the miko and the councillors of the village in recognition of distinguished services on the war-path. There was but one "great warrior" in each group, and to achieve this office was the height of every young brave's ambition. Where several villages united in a campaign a head war-chief was appointed for the emergency. An intermediate privileged class of men ranked between the councillors and the common people, their functions being mainly of an advisory character, or in connection with the elab-orate ceremonials of the tribe.

The houses which composed the Creek villages were arranged in groups or clusters, each group oc-cupied by a single clan. In or near the centre of the village was the public square, which contained the "Great House" and the "Council House" and was in addition the playground of the town. The great house was in the centre of the square and composed of four single-storied buildings facing inward and enclosing a court thirty feet square. The buildings were sheds constructed of wooden frames covered in with roughhewn slabs, and each house was divided into three compartments with platforms or bunks running around the sides. They were all open towards the central court, and each building seems to have been assigned to one of the classes mentioned above. From the roofs hung trophies of various sorts, and in the centre of the square a perpetual fire was kept burning by special attendants appointed for the purpose. The great house was the centre for all meetings of a public character, the place for holding the annual "busk," presently to be described, as well as for the daily dances and amusements. Visiting Indians were also entertained in the great house.

The council house stood on a circular mound near one corner of the great house. It was built in the shape of a large cone, placed on walls about twelve feet high, and was from twenty-five to thirty feet in diameter. Here the miko and the council met for deliberations of a private or formal character, but when not officially in use it was a general meeting-place for various purposes.

The religious and ceremonial life of the Creek concentrated in the annual festival of the *puskita*, or busk, or green - corn dance, as it has come to be

called in English. In the larger villages it lasted
eight days and its date depended upon the ripening
of the maize. The chief features were the ceremonial making of new fire by friction in the central square of the great house, the drinking of the
"black drink" (decoction of *Iris versicolor*), the
dances of a symbolic character on successive days,
and rigid abstinence from food, followed at the end
of the busk by feasting and dancing of the wildest
kind. It is usually considered that the ceremonial was in honor of the sun as the giver of the
new fruits of the year, the sun being symbolized
by the fire burning in the court. The new fire ex-
emplified the new life, physical and moral, which
was to begin with the new year. The fasting fitted
the people for this new life, and the conviviality
at the close expressed the idea that all men are
brothers. The black drink was the symbol of
purification and absolution from sin and offences
of all sorts.[1]

It is always as dangerous as it is enticing to trace
the symbolism of primitive ceremonials. Whether
all these motives were present in the Creek mind it is
impossible to say. One thing is certain, and that
is that the busk did exert a most salutary effect
upon the participants. Quarrels and feuds were
forgotten and never revived, and, except for murder,
amnesty was declared for all crimes. Houses were
refurbished, utensils and clothing were made anew,

---

[1] Gatschet, *Migration Legend of the Creek Indians*, 182.

and a fresh start was undertaken by all the members of the tribe.

There is much in the Creek organization that suggests the Iroquois, but there are also very marked dissimilarities. In the social order of the Iroquois the woman held a conspicuous and honorable position; among the Creek, in spite of strict maternal inheritance, her individual position was subordinate. She was not allowed to participate, except in a most modest manner, in the busk, nor was she permitted to be present at the councils. Her occupations were, in general, the household duties assigned to her sex among all Indian tribes.

The union of these numerous Creek villages or tribes for purposes of defence is usually called the Creek confederacy, but its structure was extremely loose as compared with the systematic working out of the Iroquois League. Each village remained strictly independent even when war had been determined upon; and not only each village but each individual was free to go upon the war-path or not as he elected.

An interesting fact regarding the procedure of these villages was the authority of the civil council in initiating military measures either of aggression or defence. The warriors were not members of the council, though the great warrior sat as a consulting officer. In spite, however, of a decision of the council in favor of peace, the great warrior might persist in "raising his hatchet" against an offending

tribe and lead those who chose to follow on the
war-path; and the council was powerless to prevent
him. In general the attitude of the Creek confederacy was strictly defensive, and when any tribe
undertook an independent offensive campaign it
was not sustained by the others. There was a
head chief of the confederacy, but he appears
to have been simply an advisory and presiding
officer without any particular position of command.

The final downfall of the Creek in the east came
about in the early part of the last century, when,
after a series of disastrous wars with the United
States, they were, in 1832, removed to Indian Territory, where they still conduct an independent government similar to that of the Cherokee.

A late offshoot of the Creek was the Seminole tribe
of Florida. Except for certain minor changes in
their industrial life, brought about by their special
habitat, what has been said of the Creek would
apply to them. Their social organization is much
the same, and the green - corn dance is their chief
ceremonial and religious expression. They are conspicuous in American history from the war which
resulted from their refusal to be removed to Indian
Territory. This struggle lasted from 1835 to 1842,
and finally resulted in the overthrow of the Seminole and their departure to Indian Territory, where
they still reside as one of the "civilized nations."
A small number remained in Florida and keep up

their old customs in the Everglades of the southern part of the peninsula.[1]

The area occupied by the Seminole in the last century was formerly the seat of the now extinct Timacua, who may be regarded as the aborigines of the Floridan peninsula. They are classed as an independent linguistic stock, but their language as recorded shows affinities both with the Carib of the West Indies and the Muskhogean.[2]

The western branch of the Muskhogean family, the Choctaw, were much less warlike and restless than the Chickasaw and Creek. They were agricultural to a high degree, depending little upon hunting for subsistence. Ethnologically the two factors of distinguishing interest about the Choctaw are their custom of flattening the heads of new-born infants by fronto-occipital pressure, and certain peculiar rites concerning the burial of the dead. The body was disinterred a short time after burial and the bones stripped of all flesh, after which they were preserved with religious care in the "bone houses" which existed in every village.[3] This latter custom was not confined to the Choctaw, but in one form or another existed among many of the eastern tribes. The neighbors of the Choctaw on the east were the Chickasaw, who differed from them

---

[1] MacCauley, "The Seminole Indians of Florida" (Bureau of Ethnology, *Fifth Annual Report*, 475).

[2] Gatschet, *Migration Legend of the Creek Indians*, 11.

[3] B. Romans, *East and West Florida*, 86, cited by Gatschet, *Migration Legend of the Creek Indians*.

very little in language and culture except in the matter of warlike proclivities mentioned above. Both tribes were organized with clans and traced inheritance through the mother; both now reside in Indian Territory as civilized tribes.

On the eastern and western borders of the Muskhogean stock were a few small tribes speaking totally distinct languages and of diverse families. In North and South Carolina were the Catawba of the Siouan family, and to the south of them the Yuchi or Uchee, an independent stock for whom thus far no affiliations whatever have been traced. Their culture was similar to that of the Creek, and the surviving remnant in Indian Territory is usually classed with that nation.

On the west as neighbors of the Choctaw were the Natchez, Tonika, and Chitimacha, all small tribes near the mouth of the Mississippi, but all speaking independent tongues. Other small stock remnants such as the Adaize, Attacapa, Karankawa, and Tonkawa bring us back to the families of the southern plains and the peculiar culture of the great southwest.

CHAPTER XII

INDIAN TRIBES OF THE SOUTHWEST AND OF MEXICO

(1500–1900)

IN the great arid stretches of the southwest appear a considerable number of tribes which may be conveniently grouped into two general classes according to their manner of living—viz., pueblo and non-pueblo peoples. The non-pueblo group includes representatives of the Athapascan, Piman, Yuman, and Shoshonean stocks. Of these the Athapascan are the most numerous and in many ways the most interesting and comprise the two well-known tribes of the Navajo and Apache. How they became separated from their kindred of the far north and how they reached their present home is one of the puzzles of American ethnology.[1]

The Navajo have an interesting legend describing their origin and early history, according to which they are not a homogeneous people but a very mixed one, containing, in addition to the original

[1] Cf. Boas, "Northern Elements in the Mythology of the Navajo" (*American Anthropologist*, X., 371); Hodge, "The Early Navajo and Apache" (*American Anthropologist*, VIII., 239).

Athapascan element, strains of Zuñian and other pueblo stocks as well as of Shoshonean and Yuman. The physical appearance of the people seems to corroborate this tradition, for it is impossible to describe a purely Navajo type. All varieties of face and figure appear, from the tall stature and prominent features of the Indians of the plains to the short body and less strongly marked lineaments of the pueblo type.[1]

The country occupied by the Navajo lies in northern Arizona and southern Utah, with the adjacent parts of Colorado and New Mexico; it is arid and in large measure desert, and consists principally of a lofty table-land, with here and there mountain-ranges or volcanic cones, broken in places by broad, sandy valleys or deep and rugged cañons. Above six to seven thousand feet the uplands and mountains are covered with low forests, while during the rainy season a rich but ephemeral vegetable growth covers the mesas; but the rainfall is too scanty to allow of agriculture, except along the few permanent streams. The country is, nevertheless, fairly well adapted to the raising of sheep and goats, of which every family now possesses a flock, and these form the chief food supply of the Navajo; though as those animals are not native to America, these people could not have been shepherds for very many centuries.

The Navajo are now, in comparison with Indians generally, a prosperous and wealthy people, but

[1] Matthews, *Navaho Legends*, 9.

their traditions indicate that they were formerly only poor hunters and lived largely upon the seeds of wild plants and upon such small animals as they trapped. To obtain pasturage for their flocks and bands of horses, they are obliged to live in small groups and lead a rather nomadic life. This has had its effect on their social organization into local groups. The lack of a definite or recognized government and authority was reflected in the difficulties experienced by the United States in its treaty negotiations with the tribe. In a few of the larger cañons, where there are small streams and patches of arable land, permanent settlements exist, seldom of more than ten or twelve families; though such places are often the scenes of large gatherings on ceremonial occasions. All cultivated or arable land is held as private property, and while the rest of the country is free to all, the rights of certain families or groups to certain localities seem to be generally recognized. In earlier times the clan organization was more compact, and the country was apportioned among the different clans, of which there were over forty; but most, if not all, of the names given to these clans are merely the designations for certain localities.[1]

The habitations[2] of the Navajo are of two sorts: a simple shelter or brush arbor used during the

[1] Matthews, *Navaho Legends*, 31.
[2] Mindeleff, "Navaho Houses" (Bureau of Ethnology, *Seventeenth Annual Report*, II.).

summer, and a more permanent lodge for the winter
months. The typical winter dwelling, or "hogan,"
is a conical structure made of stout poles inclining
inward at an angle of about forty-five degrees and
covered with bark and earth. A doorway something like a dormer-window is constructed on one
side, and in cold weather is covered with a blanket
or skin; and an opening for the escape of smoke is
left at the top. These houses average about seven
feet high by fourteen feet in diameter. When long
poles can be obtained "medicine lodges" are built,
similar in structure but larger. In other places the
medicine lodges are constructed on a rude frame with
walls and roof separate, presenting an appearance
somewhat like that of the earth lodges of the Mandan.

The house and all that it contains, aside from
the husband's weapons and personal possessions,
belong by common consent to the wife. Neither
has the husband any claim upon whatever sheep,
horses, or fields the wife may have acquired by inheritance or purchase. The children belong wholly
to the mother and to her clan, and she assumes the
entire direction of the house life. It is the duty of
the men to do most of the field-work, and most of
them are active workers, the care of their fields,
flocks, and herds demanding considerable attention.
Within recent times many of the Navajo men have
become expert silversmiths.[1] The women are also

[1] Matthews, "Navajo Silversmiths" (Bureau of Ethnology,
Second Annual Report).

very industrious, spinning, weaving, and knitting, taking most of the time they can spare from household duties. The Navajo blankets are justly famed for their durability, fineness of finish, beauty of design, and variety of pattern. The manufacture of pottery is on the decline, and most of the baskets in use among the Navajo have been obtained from other tribes.

Their mythology is very complex and their religious practices and beliefs are difficult to comprehend. They have a large number of ceremonies, some of which are long and elaborate, and all ostensibly for the cure of some sick person, and conducted by the shaman or medicine-man. In connection with these, very elaborate sand mosaics or paintings, depicting mystic emblems and groups of various deities, are made of dry sand of different colors, of charcoal, and of ochres. A considerable part of the rites consists in dancing and the singing of sacred songs, which vary for each ceremonial. They have in addition, for every important act of their lives, from birth to death, songs or poems, as they might be called, which may be numbered by the thousand, handed down from generation to generation. These rites and ceremonies, while less elaborate than those of the Pueblos, show general resemblance, which suggests the possibility that they are borrowed. The differences are marked enough, however, to indicate fairly that the Navajos have held independent development for a considerable period, even though their ceremonies may come from the same source as those of their near neighbors.

The Apache, already mentioned as belonging to the Athapascan stock, formerly lived in southeastern Arizona and southwestern New Mexico, and ranged over the surrounding country. They are divided into various groups, including the Mescalero, Jicarilla, Lipan (sometimes regarded as separate tribes), Coyotero, White Mountain Apache, etc. Most of the Apache at present have stock, and raise small quantities of corn and melons; but they still subsist largely on wild seeds and fruits, as well as on grain when they can obtain it. They are skilled in the making of baskets and water-bottles, the latter coated with piñon gum to make them watertight. They have always been a warlike and predatory people and still retain much of their original disposition.

Of the Yuman stock there are several tribes in western Arizona and southern and Lower California, including the Mohave, Maricopa, Seri, Havasupai, etc. The picturesque home of the Havasupai lies at the bottom of Cataract Cañon on a tributary of the Colorado. The widening of the cañon leaves a narrow strip of land between the stream and the lofty walls which tower hundreds of feet high. Here, by a careful system of irrigation are raised corn, melons, pumpkins, beans, peaches, etc., which flourish in great profusion in the almost tropical heat. Old houses are found on the cliffs along the walls of the cañon, which according to tradition were once occupied by certain families; hence it is probable that in early days the Havasupai were cliff-dwellers.[1]

The term "pueblo," a Spanish word meaning village, has come into general use as the name both for a certain kind of Indian town or village found in the southwest and for the inhabitants of those villages as well. The pueblos are of the communal type, the houses rising from one to five or six stories in height and arranged along more or less irregular passageways or courts. They are usually substantially built of adobe or of stone laid in a clay mortar, with square or rectangular rooms and flat roofs. The larger buildings rise like terraces, the upper stories being reached from the roof of the one next below. Formerly at least, the lower tier of rooms was entered from above from the first terrace, which was reached by ladders which could be pulled up in times of danger; there were no doors on the ground floor. Since the danger of hostile attacks has ceased doors are very frequently made opening on the street. While some of the pueblos are situated on the plain, others are placed on lofty heights which can only be reached by steep and difficult trails.

About the middle of the sixteenth century the number of pueblos was estimated at sixty-five; at

[1] Cushing, "The Nation of the Willows" (*Atlantic Monthly*, L., 362–374, 541–559).

present there are only twenty - seven inhabited
pueblos, with a population of about ten thousand;
and but few of these are supposed to be the same
as those found by the Spanish explorers.[1] Many
attempts have been made to identify the sites of
the villages known to these early travellers, but
most of them are still in doubt, except Acoma and
the Hopi towns. The present pueblos, though exhibiting practically the same culture, are distributed between four different linguistic stocks: the
Tanoan, the Keresan, the Zuñian, and the Shoshonean. The Tanoan is the largest, comprising twelve
villages: Taos, Picuris, Tesuque, Santa Clara, San
Juan, San Ildefonso, Jemez, Sandia, Nambe, Isleta
(New Mexico), Isleta (Texas), Senecu (Mexico), and
Tewa or Hano, all but the last three on the upper
Rio Grande in New Mexico. Hano is one of the
Hopi towns in Arizona, and was settled by people
who fled from the Rio Grande for fear of Spanish
vengeance after the native uprising of 1680.

The seven Keresan villages are Chochiti, San
Felipe, Santa Ana, Santo Domingo, Sia, Laguna,
and Acoma, all situated along the Rio Grande or its
tributaries and south of most of the Tanoan towns.
Zuñi, the only permanently inhabited village of the
Zuñian stock, is farther west, near the Arizona
border. Of Shoshonean stock are six of the seven

[1] Bandelier, "Historical Introduction to Studies among the
Sedentary Indians of New Mexico" (Archæological Institute
of America, *Papers*, I., 1–33).

Hopi or Moki towns in northwestern Arizona—namely, Mashongnivi, Shumopovi, Shupaulovi, Sichumovi, Oraibi, and Walpi. Connected with certain of these towns, especially Zuñi, Laguna, and Acoma, are a number of summer pueblos which are inhabited during the farming season, as they are nearer the fields, and hence eliminate the long journeys that must be taken morning and night by those living in the older towns. These may in time become permanent villages, as there is no longer anywhere necessity for protection from attack which the larger towns afforded.

Physically, the Pueblo Indians are of short stature, with long, low head, delicate face, and dark skin. They are muscular and of great endurance, able to carry heavy burdens up steep and difficult trails, and to walk or even run great distances. It is said to be no uncommon thing for a Hopi to run forty miles over a burning desert to his cornfield, hoe his corn, and return home within twenty-four hours. Distances of one hundred and forty miles are frequently made within thirty-six hours.[1] In disposition they are mild and peaceable, industrious, and extraordinarily conservative, a trait shown in the fidelity with which they retain and perpetuate their ancient customs.

Though the region inhabited by these peoples is arid, their main dependence is on agriculture. Fields of corn, melons, squashes, beans, chile, tobacco, etc.,

[1] James, *Indians of the Painted Desert*, 90.

as well as orchards of peaches, are found in the neighborhood of most of the pueblos. There is often a system of irrigation, and dams are built for the storage of water, not only for irrigating purposes, but also for domestic use. The fields are frequently at a distance of many miles from the village; for land with a sufficient amount of moisture to produce crops can be found only at scattered spots.

In addition to looking after the fields, the men do the spinning, weaving, knitting, and making of garments of cotton and wool, cotton having been raised by the Pueblo Indians from prehistoric times. They also have to procure fuel, which must often be brought from far-distant points. The women, on the other hand, not only own the house, as among the Navajo, but also do the building, though it is the duty of the men to supply the larger wooden rafters and beams. The women must also carry the water, which in the case of those living on high elevations, like the Hopi, is no easy task. The grinding of meal and preparing of food take a large portion of their time. In addition to this they make the pottery, for which the Pueblo region has become famous.[1]

The social organization is by villages rather than

[1] Holmes, "Pottery of the Ancient Pueblos" (Bureau of Ethnology, *Fourth Annual Report*); Cushing, "A Study of Pueblo Pottery" (*ibid.*); Fewkes, "Archæological Expedition to Arizona" (*ibid., Seventeenth Annual Report*); Hough, "Archæological Field-Work in Northeastern Arizona" (U. S. National Museum, *Report for 1901*).

tribes, each pueblo having a peace-chief or governor, with a number of councillors, and a war-chief. The clans,[1] which are very numerous in proportion to the population, are at the basis of the entire social and religious organization. Marriage is monogamous, and the children belong to the clan of the mother, the daughters inheriting the mother's personal possessions. Private property in land is not recognized, though individual occupation is respected as long as the land is in use.

The Pueblo, as a rule, are very religious, much of their time being spent in elaborate ceremonials. The performance of these ceremonies and rites is in the hands of secret societies or priesthoods, of which there are several in every village. These have been studied in a number of villages, but probably those of the Hopi or Moki are the best known. Here from four to sixteen days in every month are employed by one society or another in the carrying out of religious rites; the public performances are inappropriately termed "dances" by the whites, as in the case of the so-called "snake-dance." The secret portion of these ceremonies takes place in the "kiva," a rectangular room, usually underground, and always entered by a trap-door in the roof. The ceremonies are very complex, some of them lasting over a week, and abound in details too long for these pages. In many cases an elaborate structure, usually called

[1] Hodge, "Pueblo Indian Clans" (*American Anthropologist*, IX., 345).

an altar, is constructed in the kiva, the chief feature
being a complicated sand mosaic, reminding one of
the sand paintings of the Navajo. Numerous symbolic figures are represented, especially the symbols
for clouds and rain, and prayer - sticks and other
objects are placed around it. Prayer-sticks are always used in connection with religious ceremonies,
for without them the supplication would be in-
effectual. In some of the ceremonies, to make the
prayers to the clan ancestors called "katcinas"
more effectual, these deities are impersonated by
men wearing masks and dressed in costumes characteristic of these beings. Nearly all of the ceremonies, though in large part secret, close with a public performance, often most brilliant and striking,
of which the snake-dance is a good example.

The purpose of these elaborate ceremonies may
be summed up in one word—rain. The very existence of the Pueblo Indian is dependent upon his
crops, of which corn is the most important. In the
arid region in which he lives it is always a question
whether the rainfall will be sufficient to bring this
to maturity. He believes that there are immense
reservoirs in the heavens where the water is stored
up, and hence every endeavor is made to gain the
favor of the powers above, who control the supply,
that they may grant him sufficient rain and a
bountiful harvest.

In Mexico and Central America appear a great
number of Indian tribes, representing numerous

linguistic stocks and all degrees of development. Some of them reached the highest stages of culture known to have existed on the western continent. Many other more primitive tribes are little known and of small historical importance; of the more significant groups the best known are doubtless the Nahua or Aztec, among the different tribes of which, some living as far south as Nicaragua and Costa Rica, the most noted composed the famous Aztec confederacy. This confederacy, with certain conquered tribes which it held in subjection, is what has been called the "empire of Montezuma." It was composed of three towns with the territories belonging to each: Tenochtitlan or Mexico, Tezcuco, and Tlacopan. Mexico or Tenochtitlan was the head of the confederacy and the seat of government.

Another people who had attained an equal and in some respects a higher degree of culture were the Maya-Quiché tribes, most of them living in Yucatan and Guatemala. Of these the Maya of Yucatan are the most important. In the region now included by the Mexican state of Michoacan and portions of some neighboring districts were found the Tarascan, who had a somewhat different culture, though still high. In Oaxaca were the Mixtec and Zapotec, of whom numerous remains are found. In Vera Cruz were the Huastec, a branch of the Maya-Quiché family. Between them and the Nahua were the Totonac, whose remains also indicate a distinct culture. These may be regarded as the most advanced in civilization of the Mexican peoples. In northern Mexico remains are found which indicate a culture intermediate between that of the Pueblo and that of the groups just mentioned.

Many of the Mexican tribes are still living under almost primitive conditions, but practically all of them have been influenced more or less by the Spaniards and by later European culture. The present descendants of the older and more civilized peoples, including approximately two million Nahua, know practically nothing of the culture of their forefathers and lead a relatively simple life, though they still cling tenaciously to many of their former customs and refuse to adopt the new civilization around them.

That a considerable advance towards civilization had been made by these peoples before the arrival of the Spaniards is indicated, not only by the accounts of their conquerors, but also by the very numerous remains that have been discovered, especially within recent years. The earlier accounts were painted in glowing colors, and while at first accepted and later discredited, are now generally believed to contain a considerable element of truth, though in many places distorted through lack of appreciation of native customs and beliefs, and in other cases exaggerated.

The most important of the remains are found on the sites of ancient cities, and the architecture of the buildings themselves is one of the most important features. The great ruins of the Nahua group include Tula, Teotihuacan, Xochicalco, Tepoztlan, Cholula, and Tenochtitlan, now the city of Mexico. Though this city was destroyed at the time of the conquest, a vast number of objects were buried beneath the soil on which the new city arose, and many of these have recently been brought to light. In the Huastecan and Totonacan regions are the ruins of Papantla, Misantla, Cuetla, Tusapan, and Cempoalla. The ruins on Monte Alban in Oaxaca are the most stupendous in all Mexico, and are supposed to represent the seat of the ancient capital of the Zapotec. Mitla, in the same district, is a noted example of ancient architecture, and in some ways the most remarkable in America. Here stones of many tons have been brought from quarries on the neighboring mountains, and all have been fitted together with the utmost nicety and precision. Here, as in many other places, complicated carved designs are found, covering whole faces of buildings, and all accomplished with nothing better than tools of stone or possibly of hardened copper.

In the Maya region are remains of hundreds of towns remarkable for their size and elaborate sculptures. Among the most important may be mentioned Palenque, Menché, Tikal, Labna, Kabah, Uxmal, Chichen Itza, Quirigua, and Copan. One feature common to most of these ruins is the presence of pyramids, frequently of immense size, and usually surmounted by buildings. In Yucatan the pyramids are usually built, or at least faced, with stone, while among the Nahua they were constructed of adobe brick. The pyramid of Cholula, originally crowned by a temple which was destroyed by Cortés, was fourteen hundred and forty feet square at the base and one hundred and seventy-seven feet high.

The civilization,[1] however, which is represented by these ancient ruins is not to be regarded as anything radically different from that we have met farther north, but rather as a development along the same lines, with modifications due to a more complex organization. There are many points in common with the Pueblo culture of the southwest: we still find the peace-chief, with his councillors, and the war-chief, though the occupants of these positions have become more conspicuous because of the increasing complexity and material prosperity of a higher state of culture. Montezuma, for example, is now known to have been simply the war-chief of the Aztec confederation, holder of an elective office, from which the chief could be deposed for misconduct—a common provision among Indian tribes, but not ordinarily compatible with hereditary

[1] Bandelier, "On the Art of War and Mode of Warfare of the Ancient Mexicans" (Peabody Museum, *Tenth Annual Report*); "On the Distribution and Tenure of Lands and the Customs with Respect to Inheritance among the Ancient Mexicans" (*ibid., Eleventh Annual Report*); "On the Social Organization and Mode of Government of the Ancient Mexicans" (*ibid., Twelfth Annual Report*).

monarchy. The clan was still the basis of the social structure, and the method of choosing chiefs and councillors was quite similar to that found among the Iroquois. Land was the property of the clan, and was assigned to the individual, who could hold it only as long as he cultivated it properly. The tribes conquered by the confederacy were required to pay tribute, which was collected by certain officials of the league and distributed between its members, Mexico getting two-fifths. The tributary tribes were also required to furnish warriors in case of need at the demand of the confederacy.

Among these peoples agriculture was still fundamental, but manufactures and trade were also considerably developed. Certain towns and regions became noted for particular products, and regular markets under governmental supervision were held in specified places. Great skill was displayed in the carving of wood, shells, and precious stones, and in gold and silver work. The products and art of the different regions were usually quite distinctive, especially in the better grades of pottery, which was often beautifully ornamented.

The religious system may also be regarded as a higher development of that found among the northern tribes. The mythology had become more systematized and the power of the priesthood had increased. The endeavor to propitiate the gods and to cause them to grant favoring rains and abundant crops is still most in evidence; but in connection with other interests and industries many new deities with their associated ceremonies and priesthoods had been introduced. The religious rites were elaborate and prescribed with minuteness, and animal and even human sacrifices were not uncommon.

Systems of picture-writing or hieroglyphics had also been developed. Among the Nahua there were numerous books, a few of which have been preserved and are still very imperfectly understood. These works, commonly called "codices," were painted on prepared paper or skins; some of them seem to be religious calendars, others historical records. The Maya had a somewhat different system of writing, of which there are a number of specimens on the monuments and a few codices. Some of these also, especially those relating to the calendar, have been partially deciphered. A third kind of inscription has recently been found in Zapotec ruins, but nothing has been accomplished in the way of interpretation. In many places wall paintings are found, which frequently remind one strongly of certain figures in the codices, which, like the figures in the sculptures, throw much light upon the dress, ornaments, and even the implements and weapons of the people.

In general it may be said that the culture of these peoples, especially of the Nahua and Maya, was much higher than that found farther north, but still a development indigenous to the country and based upon elements held in common with many other American tribes.

On the high plateaus of South America a considerable advance towards civilization had also been made, but not equal to that found in Mexico.   It is also to be regarded as a higher development, under favorable conditions, of a local culture in no wise essentially different from that of surrounding tribes.

CHAPTER XIII

SOCIAL ORGANIZATION OF THE INDIANS
(1500–1900)

THE most significant factor in Indian sociology is undoubtedly the clan. This is a kinship group in which the degree of relationship between the members is not regarded. The fact of kinship is, however, whether traceable or not, always assumed and is indispensable for the clan conception. Discussion as to the origin of the clan system has been active for many years and shows no sign of abating: a common view is that the clan is an outgrowth of the family; but there are many facts to support the contention that the family is a new formation within the clan.

Though actual kinship between members of the same clan need not necessarily be traceable, there must be some mode of expressing the idea of kinship which dominates and binds the group together, and the usual mode is the custom or institution of totemism. A totem is a class of objects, usually animals or plants, with which an individual regards himself as standing in a special relation.[1] This

---

[1] Fraser, in *Encyclopædia Britannica*, art., " Totemism."

relation may be one of descent from or kindred with the particular animal or plant, or there may be no notion of consanguinity. All those who claim this special relationship with a given totem are regarded as kin and as standing in the same degree of kinship to each other. This totemic clan is a fundamental Indian institution, and appears everywhere in North America, except in the far north, on the plateaus, at certain points on the Pacific coast, and among a few tribes of the plains.

Alongside the numerous important features of the clan organization, which vary in detail in different parts of the continent, stands out the principle that each clansman has a double relationship: a religious one to his totem, and a social one to his fellow - members of the group. Perhaps the most striking feature of the social aspect, a feature which is inflexible and shows no tendency to variation, is the law of exogamy with respect to the clan: members of the same totem group must not marry; violation of this rule was ordinarily punished with death.

Since the parents of an Indian could not be of the same clan, it was necessary for one of them to be disregarded in determining the clan or totem of the new-born child; and it was generally the father who was passed over, and the child was assigned to the clan of the mother. This is "female inheritance," and is a custom from which much has been inferred with regard to the early development of the family.

The classical deduction is that descent through the mother argues a previous condition of sexual promiscuity in which the paternity of a child would be uncertain and he must necessarily be assigned to his mother alone; with increasing stability in the marriage relation paternity would come to be reasonably certain, and the child would tend to be assigned to the father, as the head of the family, and to the father's clan where there was a clan organization. Under this theory maternal inheritance is therefore regarded as preceding, in the evolution of the family and society, the paternal recognition.

The fundamental error in this plausible line of argument, as applied to the world in general, lies in the disturbing fact that society is so complex in the factors which have contributed to its growth that it is by no means certain that what may be true of the development of an institution in one region will hold good for the entire human race. In the present chaotic condition of sociological and ethnological data it is unsafe to assert that a given tribe on a paternal basis represents a higher stage of social evolution than one on a maternal system, even though it may ultimately prove that in general the reasoning outlined above holds good. For example, as has been stated,[1] the Kwakiutl of Vancouver Island are in a transition stage from paternal to maternal institutions instead of the reverse, which should be the case according to rule.

[1] See above, chap. vii.

Whatever the reason, the majority of the Indian tribes traced descent through the mother, and children were assigned to the mother's clan. In some groups, where the system was less rigid, the child might, for sufficient reasons, be entered in the father's clan, even when he would normally inherit that of his mother. This would occur in cases where the paternal group was in need of strengthening. If the rules of exogamy were all, the clan organization would not be so important a factor. As a matter of fact, it enters every phase of the Indian's life: his first obligation is to his clan, and where its welfare comes into collision with that of the immediate family the latter gives way.

The wide-spread custom of "blood revenge" was a clan matter. The entire kinship group of the murdered man demanded satisfaction, and the entire clan of the murderer was held responsible. The logical extension of this conception of common blood is seen in certain South American tribes, where if an individual by accident injures himself he is obliged to pay blood-money to his clan because he has been guilty of shedding the blood of his clan.[1] A real difficulty occurred where an individual murdered a fellow-clansman, which act is in general among savages the most heinous crime of which one can be guilty, being both a sacrilegious as well as a social offence. To put the offender to death would be to commit a second crime of the same

[1] Sievers, *Reise in der Sierra Nevada de Santa Marta*, 256.

character. In certain groups the condition was cleverly met by first formally outlawing or expelling the murderer from the clan, after which he could legitimately be hunted down and put to death;[1] in other places the tendency seems to have been rather to condone the offence, as if in bewilderment as to the appropriate action.[2]

The civil functions of the clan are more important than those more purely social.[3] In most of the tribes chieftainship and special governmental privileges resided permanently in certain clans. There were ordinarily among the Indians chiefs of two kinds, who have come to be termed "sachems" and ordinary "chiefs." The sachem was essentially a civil officer and his duties and authority were confined to times of peace; while the chief might have duties concerned with war or any other affairs for which he was peculiarly fitted. The sachem was primarily an officer of the clan, and the position was hereditary in that group; a vacancy in the office was filled by election as often as it occurred. In tribes with maternal inheritance a brother or a sister's son was usually chosen to succeed a deceased sachem, though any male member of the clan was regarded as eligible. This right of election, and the corresponding right of deposition for cause,

---

[1] Cf. Powell, "Wyandot Government" (Bureau of Ethnology, *First Annual Report*, 67).

[2] Charlevoix, *Histoire de la Nouvelle France*, 274.

[3] For a masterly discussion of this whole subject and the topics which follow, see Morgan, *Ancient Society*, 62 ff.

were jealously guarded by the clans, and are the germs of democracy as expressed by the American aborigines. Among the Iroquois, however, the tribe occasionally stepped in and deposed a sachem for unworthy behavior, without waiting for the action of the clan. In such cases the latter appears to have been powerless to resist.

The term "chief," as applied to leading men among the Indians, is so indefinite as to be almost meaningless. There was, however, one qualification of great significance—namely, personal fitness. There were, in other words, chiefs rather than chieftainships, since personal prowess or ability were the conditions of the position, and the office usually died with the holder. The number of chiefs in a clan, or in a tribe without clans, was quite indefinite and depended much upon the personnel of the group. In stocks such as the Iroquois there was one chief to about every seventy-five or one hundred persons, but this cannot be taken as a criterion. In tribes with well-organized councils one of the main functions of the chief was to sit officially as a member of that body. In other more loosely constructed tribes, such as appear in the west, his duties and authority were very indefinite.

There is much misconception regarding Indian chieftainship in general. The chief was the preeminent figure only in times of great emergency, such as war; and as those were precisely the occasions upon which the Indians were usually seen by the

whites, an exaggerated idea of the chief's importance has grown up. With the passing of the
emergency the chief tended to lapse back to the
level of the other members of the tribe, and special
authority often did not exist for him. The Indian
is essentially individualistic and will not brook
authority except where long-continued custom has
proven its necessity. On the northwest coast, the
essential condition of chieftainship is wealth, which
is acquired for the purpose of making great feasts
and gifts and thereby attaining increased rank
in the order of nobles or chiefs. There is in that
region, too, a sharp line drawn between the social
classes, which makes it almost impossible for a ple-
beian, and quite so for a slave, to rise to the rank
of chief. These social differences do not appear so
much in manner of life or in the intercourse of every
day as in ceremonials and in questions of marriage.

In Indian society, therefore, the privileges pertaining to the clan were the main heritage of any
individual — name, position, and ceremonial rights
were perhaps the most valued of all these privileges;
but that of ownership of property as such seems
often to depend upon the clan organization. Where
clans existed, land was the common property of
that group; where clans were absent it belonged
to the band or tribe. It is said that in certain
regions of the northwest individual proprietorship
existed in the case of fishing and hunting locations,
but such a condition was exceptional.

The combination of common ownership and universal hospitality made the accumulation of personal property unnecessary and unusual, so that the disposition of the goods and chattels of the deceased individual did not raise a question of much importance. It was, however, bound to arise, and, as might be expected, it appears to have been the clan in which the right of inheritance lay. The most cherished and intimate of the personal effects were ordinarily buried with the deceased. The rest of his personal property went to his nearest of kin, but remained within the clan. In a maternal group a man's brothers and sisters and maternal uncles were usually his heirs; his children took nothing, since they belonged to a different clan. In the case of a woman's death her children received the bulk of her property; husband or wife inherited nothing from the other. It appears as if the individual or the family were thus the custodian rather than the actual owner of the estate.

A striking characteristic of Indian society, and one difficult for us to understand, is the great stress laid upon the name. In most groups certain names resided in certain clans and were used by no others, so that the personal name of an individual was indicative of the clan to which he belonged. The customs relating to name giving and acquisition varied widely in North America, but it was not usual for a person to receive his adult name, the one by which he would afterwards be known, until puberty, or until he had gained the right to bear it by some act of distinguished prowess or service.   In certain regions, as in the northwest, ceremonial privileges go with the name, and the right of bestowal is vested in the hereditary owner or custodian.   Under such conditions the name becomes true property and the regard for it is much more than a mere matter of sentiment.   Among the Kwakiutl a man who is in financial difficulties and unable to meet his potlatch obligations may even pawn his name for a longer or shorter period, and an excessive rate of interest is charged for the accommodation.[1]   During such time as his name is thus in pawn he must not use it in any way, and his social position is thereby lowered.   It is, further, during that period the property of the money - lender, and his position is heightened by whatever the value or rank of the pledged name may be.

Among nearly all tribes the acquisition or change of names was a matter of public ceremonial, and was regarded as an event of prime importance in the life of the individual.   Occasionally a name would be discarded after a severe illness or other misfortune, but among the eastern tribes at least such action required the consent of the clan.   Names might also be lent as a mark of particular favor or friendship, the beneficiary having the privilege of

[1] Boas, *Social Organization of the Kwakiutl Indians*, 341.

using it for a limited time, or for life, as the case might be.

One of the chief concerns of the clan was to keep and increase its strength. Under the conditions of almost unceasing warfare in which the Indians lived, the loss of members by death was a constant menace to the life and vitality of the clan. To meet this danger grew up the custom of adoption. An adopted person became in every sense a member of the clan or family or tribe into which he was received. The strangers thus adopted were, as a rule, captives in war or stray members of other tribes. The act was carried out by an individual, but had to be ratified by the clan, and sometimes by the tribe, in a ceremonial manner. Adoption was also a means of atoning for accidental homicide, and thus avoiding blood revenge. The offender in such a case would offer himself, for example, to the mother of his victim, and, being accepted by her, would assume in every form the duties and obligations of the dead son.

The settlement of disputes and all matters of debate which pertained to the clan exclusively were in the hands of the chiefs, or when they could not decide, devolved upon the council. This institution of the council was again practically universal among the Indians. Its structure might vary from that of the Iroquois clan, where the women had an equal right with men, to that of tribes of the west, where the former were not consulted; but it was

always pre-eminently a place of free speech. Its
deliberations were calm and unhurried and its deci-
sions were usually accepted without question. This
latter fact is surprising when we remember that little or no provision was made for the execution of
its decrees. As was noted in the case of the Iroquois,
the council depended upon public opinion for support and was seldom disappointed. The council
of the clan was the prototype of that of the tribe or
confederacy where such existed. Where clans were
absent the local band or tribe held its council in
the same way and to the same ends. It was the
corner-stone of Indian civil procedure, and will be
discussed again presently in connection with the
larger organizations.

These, then, are the main features of the clan as
it is found in America. It must be remembered,
however, that, hampered as the Indian might be by
tradition, by custom, by clan or other obligation, he
always insisted upon and retained his formal freedom of action. His sachems and his chiefs were his
representatives and leaders in times of emergency,
but except in such regions as the northwest coast
equality and independence were the characteristics
of American savage life.

A social institution of some importance was
slavery, which has several times been mentioned
in connection with the tribes of the Pacific coast,
where the institution found its stronghold. Captives in war were the usual victims, but their

children were also doomed to slavery, and the consequence was the formation of a class in the community as distinct as that of the nobility and nearly as permanent. While these slaves were the absolute property of their owners, and could be sold or put to death at will, their life does not appear to have been particularly hard except in unusual cases. The every-day life of the owners was not such as to permit much lowering without extinction, and the slave had about the same food and shelter as his master. Slavery of a sort also existed in the southeast; and in more modern times certain of the Muskhogean tribes, imitating the whites, became the owners of negroes.

The clans of any given tribe were ordinarily gathered into two or more classes known as phratries, which were also exogamous groups and still further restricted the choice of the individual in marriage. The phratry was probably an overgrown clan which had become unwieldy, and upon subdivision the constituent groups still retained a memory of their mutual relationship and consequent inability to intermarry. The functions of the phratry are somewhat indefinite but are distinctly social and ceremonial rather than governmental. It is seen at its best among the tribes of the east and in Mexico, but is also present in Alaska and British Columbia as well as in certain parts of the western United States.

Among the Algonquian and Iroquoian Indians the phratry appears most prominently in such social affairs as public games. In ball-games, for example, the phratries are pitted against each other and the clan disappears in the united enthusiasm. In councils of the tribe the sachems and chiefs sat by phratries and not by clans, but this arrangement was purely formal and without real significance. Among the Iroquois the influence of the phratry was sometimes invoked by a constituent clan to arrange the condonation of a murder or other offence, and often with a successful result which might not have been reached had the clan acted independently. At the funerals of important persons the phratry also appeared prominently. The members of the phratry of the deceased were the mourners, and the opposite phratry took charge of the ceremonies.

In matters of government the phratry had the right of confirming or rejecting an election of sachem or chief made by the clan. Following such an election among the Iroquois, councils of both phratries were called and each acted upon the choice. If either phratry refused to acquiesce in the nomination it was thereby null and void, and the clan was obliged to proceed to a second election. If both phratries approved the choice it was regarded as final.

In Mexico, among the Aztec, the phratry seems to have had a distinct military function as well as

to have been a social and religious group.[1]   The
warriors of the tribe were divided into four bands,
each corresponding to a phratry and each under the
leadership of a phratry captain.   Such a military
subdivision was probably not present, however, in
any of the northern tribes.

The next step in the social organization of the
Indians was the tribe.   It has already been remarked that this is an indefinite term, referring
sometimes to a single village and sometimes to a
number of such local groups.   In certain stocks
where the social system is closely knit there is no
difficulty in drawing the tribal lines.   In others,
where the organization is looser—for example, on
the plateaus — definition becomes difficult if not
impossible.   The features which are generally regarded as characteristic of a tribe, in distinction to
any other group, larger or smaller, are the possession
of a dialect and territory, and sometimes of a name
and separate government.[2]   Of these characteristics
the dialect may be regarded as determinant.   Continuity of territory will, naturally, exist for the
tribe in the vast majority of cases, since geographical
separation of related bands is exactly the factor
which tends to bring about dialectic as well as
general independence, and hence favors the formation of new tribes.

[1] Bandelier, "On the Art of War and Mode of Warfare of the
Ancient Mexicans" (Peabody Museum, *Tenth Annual Report*).
[2] Morgan, *Ancient Society*, 102.

It is impossible to lay down a strict criterion for drawing the line between tribe and band, but there is no doubt that the linguistic consideration is the most important. The habit of authorities in the case of Indian tribes has been to follow the native usage, and where the Indians recognized relationship and grouped themselves under a given name, to regard that particular aggregation as a distinct tribe. Common customs will also aid in the determination of the tribal limits, particularly where the clan organization exists and where the exogamous and endogamous regulations can be clearly stated. On the other hand a supreme government cannot be regarded as distinctive, since in many groups recognized by every one as tribes there are any number of smaller component groups or bands, each of which is entirely independent in every sense of the word.[1] Such a condition may be seen among the Shahaptian tribes of the west, as well as in other regions.[2] The few cases in which the above-mentioned characteristics of common dialect and common institutions do not occur are temporary conditions, where one tribe may be undergoing absorption by another.

It appears as if there had been a constant tendency towards disintegration among the Indian tribes; and the process was no doubt hastened by the chances for segmentation due to the wide

[1] Morgan regards the central government as distinctive; see *Ancient Society*, 102.   [2] See above, chap. viii.

geographical dispersion of certain groups. The physical features of the continent and the exigencies of the food quest are enough to account for the process. The development of agriculture doubtless tended to arrest the dispersion, since it immediately increased the number of individuals who were able to obtain subsistence from a given area; but it could never have proved more than a temporary check. The point of greatest significance in the present discussion is the place of the tribe in the development of government; and, as was brought out in the last chapter, those tribes organized on a basis of clans are the ones in which the evolution towards confederation and centralization seem to have taken place most clearly.

While in most tribes the right of electing sachems and chiefs pertained to the clan, certain tribes— *e.g.*, the Iroquois, demanded the privilege of ratification of such elections. This meant that a chief-elect was not recognized officially until ceremonially invested with authority by the council of the tribe, and unfit elections could be and were nullified by tribal action. The right of deposition for cause, which was also held by the tribe as well as by the clan, was a further safeguard in insuring good behavior after election.

Undoubtedly, the most interesting development of the tribe was the council of chiefs, which was organized on much the same plan as that of the clan. Chiefs of the clans, where such existed, were

ex-officio members of the tribal council, and that body
held ultimate authority over tribal affairs. The
democratic spirit was evident here as well as in the
clan, since the meetings of the council were open to
address by any adult male member of the tribe; and
among the Iroquois any woman could express her
views through an orator chosen by herself. The
tribal council determined upon military campaigns,
had the power to make peace, and conducted all
negotiations with other tribes.

A head chief of the tribe did not exist as a rule;
though in certain cases one of the sachems was
recognized as of higher rank and authority than
the others, and upon him would devolve the duty
of representing the tribe when the council was not
or could not be convened. In such circumstances
his action was always subject to ratification by the
council, and his authority depended almost wholly
upon his personal capacity and influence. The
early designation of some of these leading chiefs as
"kings" is absurd, as there was little in the position
of an executive character. Among the Aztec the
head war - chief, Montezuma, naturally became a
figure of prominence owing to the necessities of the
military situation at the time of the Spanish invasion; but among the tribes farther north the so-
called king was nothing more than the elective and
often temporary chief of a tribe, or possibly of a
confederation. Among the Iroquois, who, as we
have seen, carried the idea of representative govern-

ment to a high degree of expression, no head chief at all was recognized.

Where segmentation, from whatever cause, has brought about the formation of new dialects and tribal bonds, the relationship between the tribes thus formed will often be recognized although the fact of former unity may not be remembered even in tradition. When to this relationship be added geographical contiguity, it is evident that the interests of the given tribes will often be common.

Among the Indi ns generally the constant fear was of attack from hostile groups, and the suggestion of union of related tribes for mutual defence would be as natural as the occasion was frequent. This was unquestionably the origin of the confederacy, which may also be regarded as a typical Indian institution. In the confederacy as well as in the tribe the clan influence persisted and was the basis of organization. In cases where clans were unknown the leagues have usually been of a more fragile and temporary character, a fact which emphasizes the importance of the kinship bond in the civil unions.

The two confederacies of highest type in North America were those of the Iroquois and the Aztec, both of which have been briefly described. Others which were of considerable permanence were the Creek, Dakota, Moki, and Blackfoot. The last-named is especially interesting, since it includes a tribe of Athapascan stock, the Sarcee, while the

other and presumably original members of the
league are of Algonquian lineage. The confederacies
to which reference is often made in the history of
the colonies and the western movement were generally temporary unions for special emergencies,
and were rather loose alliances than true confederations. Such, for example, were the various
leagues among the tribes of New England, the
Powhatan in Virginia, the Illinois in the state of
that name, and others.

One of the most valuable results of modern
ethnological research is the proof, now indisputa-
ble, that practically all of these confederacies were
similar in general character. The reaction from
the extravagances and inaccuracies of the Spánish
recorders and their later interpreters produced a
swing of the pendulum of authority which reduced
the Aztec to the level of the Mohawk, and be-
littled the advances in all directions which the
Mexicans and Maya had achieved. The more moderate opinion is probably correct — viz., that the
Aztec political and industrial systems had developed further, but along much the same lines, as in
the more northern tribes.

The process and to a certain extent the causes
of the higher attainments of the Aztec are not hard
to understand. The development of agriculture by
the elaboration of irrigation naturally produced a
greater density of population. With the increasing numbers in a limited area organization became

a necessity. The pressure on the food supply brought about a system of organized plunder from tribes which had been conquered and were held in subjugation by the efficiency of the confederation. The collection of this tribute and its equable distribution demanded an executive, and it was provided by increased dignity and authority vested in the war-chief, who was gradually assuming civil as well as military functions. Coincident with this growth of the chief executive, which must be considered the most significant phase of the Aztec government, came an increase in the number of subordinate civil officers and consequent differentiation in their functions. It is not unlikely that with time the two war-chiefships of the Iroquois,[1] created for special military operations, would have been consolidated and a more permanent executive with civil functions have been developed. In other words, the Iroquois were probably following the very course of civil evolution through which the Aztec had already passed, though the progress was necessarily slower, by reason of the local dispersion of the former as compared with the compact village communities of the latter.

[1] See above, chap. x.

CHAPTER XIV

INDIAN HOUSES, HOUSE LIFE, AND FOOD QUEST

(1500–1900)

TWO facts stand out clearly from the earliest authentic information regarding the Indians: the first is that the continent was sparsely settled in pre-Columbian times; the second that the inhabitants were sedentary rather than nomadic in manner of life. The fact that Indians were everywhere encountered by the early settlers means nothing, except that the same natural features which attracted the white attracted the Indian as well. Practically everywhere the natives were gathered together in villages, the sites of which were determined by natural advantages. These villages were almost invariably small, seldom with more than a few hundred inhabitants, and usually with less. With the inevitable growth and extension of these groups new villages were formed, the inhabitants of which naturally retained dialectic and cultural affiliations, and thus afforded an opportunity for the confederations which were brought about by common interests. Language and geographical proximity were the pre-eminent factors in binding together the tribes and confederacies.

Furthermore, these villages were almost always permanent, although the seasonal changes of residence brought about by the necessities of the food quest often gave to the early observers the impression of an unstable and nomadic habit. Scattered at intervals along the coasts of both oceans, and on the waterways of the continent and about the shores of the lakes of the interior, it is not strange that the white immigrants encountered these villages at every turn and supposed that the vast intervening territories were as thickly peopled as the natural routes of travel which they happened to be following; whereas, as a matter of fact, large areas were nearly as destitute of Indian as of white inhabitants.

For this and other reasons, gross misconceptions have arisen regarding the number of Indians at the discovery; and with them equally erroneous ideas as to the rapid decrease and inevitable extinction of the race.[1] Such calculations as can be made would show nothing but a gradual diminishing of their numbers, except in special groups; and in some cases an increase can be proven. So far as the evidence is attainable, it indicates that sparse and scattered population has been the condition from time immemorial.

[1] See above, chap. vi.

To return to the villages—the dwellings of which they consisted naturally varied widely in character both with the environment and with the culture and social organization of the inhabitants. The architectural characteristics show many variations and are not distributed with geographical regularity; some of the most characteristic types have been described in the preceding chapters, and we need do nothing more than sum up at this point. The most widely distributed Indian houses were undoubtedly the light and not very durable shelters of brush, bark, and skin. These were sometimes elaborate, like the Iroquois "long houses," or rude and simple, like the "wickiups" of the southern Shoshone.

The bark and brush wigwams which are regarded as typical of the eastern tribes were, however, permanent dwellings, and were modified by the buffalo-hunting and rapidly moving Indians of the plains to meet their own conditions. These conditions brought about the device of the tipi already described,[1] which has been adopted so widely in the open country of the west. On the border between the eastern and western group one of those curious transitions in type is sometimes seen, such as a wigwam built on tipi lines or a tipi adapted to the woodland life. The eastern Sioux construct a lodge of bark like the Iroquois, but with far less skill and finish. Lodges covered in with woven

[1] See above, chap. ix.

mats were also common in many tribes, but usually as summer shelters. The Nez Percé of Idaho were described by the early explorers as living in houses as much as one hundred and fifty feet in length and built of straw and mats, the idea having been borrowed, it was supposed, from the wooden houses of the Pacific coast. The evidence is fairly good, however, that such were not the common Shahaptian dwellings but sporadic foreign introductions.

The simpler type of the more permanent dwellings is seen in the underground lodges of the northwestern plateaus, which were devised to afford protection in the severe winters of that region, and are simply a modification of the more temporary shelters of brush and bark just described. A shallow excavation, circular in form, was covered in with a conical roof of poles, and that with brush or mats, and often with earth. These earth houses are typically western and appear chiefly on the plateaus, in Oregon and central California, on the southern plains, and in the southwest, among such tribes as the Navajo and Pomo. They occur sporadically, but not generally, in other parts of the continent. The details of construction vary: they are sometimes round, sometimes square, sometimes large, and sometimes small, but almost always embody the three features of excavation, particularly where the winters are hard; of a frame-work of poles or beams; and of a covering of earth or sod. The snow houses of the Eskimo are adaptations of the same idea to their frozen environment, but the rafters are lacking and the blocks of snow are wedged tight by the key-block at the summit of the rounded arch.

The greatest development of wooden houses, that of the northwest coast, has already been described.[1] In that region the attempt was made to roughhew the planks, but in other parts of the continent wooden houses were usually built of poles, or sometimes, as among the Cherokee, of logs.

The highest form of native architecture is reached in the southwestern states and in Mexico. Within the limits of the United States the Pueblo dwellings of Arizona and New Mexico are the best and most durable. The typical Pueblo village is a cluster of rectangular houses, or rather rooms, arranged about a central court, or in a row, and usually placed one over the other in terraces. The walls of the older Pueblo houses are of undressed stone, and the roofs are formed of beams, with successive layers of smaller sticks, brush, and packed earth. Ladders give access to the terraces, and the rooms of the ground floor were entered by holes in the roof. In these modern days, doors, stone stairways, chimneys, and drains are being introduced with rapidity, and modify the more primitive character of the houses.

The ancient cliff-dwellings of the cañons were nothing more than these Pueblo houses built in

[1] See above, chap. iii.

great niches of the cañon walls, with the overhanging cliffs to give protection and incidentally to preserve the ruins. There is good evidence that they are no older in type than the Pueblo houses of to-day, and that they were contemporaneous with the villages built on the flats. It is also thought by some writers that the peculiar elevated sites were not chosen primarily for purposes of defence, but simply as affording favorable lookout places during the seasons when the fields were in cultivation. Doubtless both considerations contributed to the choice of site.

The massive architectural remains of Mexico and Central America can only be mentioned. They unquestionably mark the apex of Indian development, and their magnificence has led to very wrong ideas as to the general level of culture to which the Aztec and their neighbors had attained. Some of these Central American structures were of enormous size, a thousand feet or more in ground diameter and as much as two hundred feet high. They were built of large blocks of stone, laid in mortar, and finished in various ways. It is a remarkable fact that with this skill in construction the principle of the arch was never used.

There can be no doubt that in the local form of Indian houses, the continent over, social organization had a determining influence.[1] The type of construction may have been the result of physical en-

[1] Morgan, *Houses and House Life.*

vironment, but the group organization undoubtedly
led to the communal houses of the Iroquois and
the Pueblo, of the Kwakiutl and the Mandan, and of
numerous other tribes as well; and where communal
houses did not exist a similar local clustering of
individual lodges on a basis of relationship tended to
appear.

Moreover, the system of social organization determined other arrangements still more domestic in
character.   The position and influence of the woman
in the "long house" of the Iroquois have been noted.
It was not an exceptional case; much nonsense has
been written and believed regarding the "squaw"
in Indian society.   She is pictured as a drudge and
slave, while her lord and master, dignified and
lazy, is supposed never to lift his hand to work
except under stress of direst necessity.   Such ideas
are very far from the truth.   The division of labor
between the sexes is not very unequal in the majority
of tribes, where the hunting-life entails prolonged
and strenuous exertion on the part of the men; and
the independence and authority of the woman in
household affairs are usually recognized and often
exerted.   The lines separating the work of the men
from that of the women are sharply drawn, and
interference from either side is seldom brooked.

The care of the lodge, preparation of food, and
making of clothing and household utensils fall to
the woman; while the arts of hunting and war, with
the manufacture of weapons, are the peculiar care of

the man.   With the inroads of civilization the labor
of the man has become less and less and his energy
has decreased at an equal rate.   The task of the
woman, on the other hand, has rather been added to
than lightened, and the disproportion thus brought
about affords a certain basis for the popular notions
on the subject.

In the every-day life of the Indian the satisfaction
of his hunger was naturally his most important need.
The means to this end were as varied as the environment in which he lived.   While it is justifiable
to speak of the Indians in general as hunting and
fishing folk, it is clear from the descriptions already
given that a large proportion of them practised
agriculture.   It was only in the north and among
some of the western tribes that hunting formed the
chief means of subsistence.   As soon as the latitude
permits the growth of berries, seeds, and edible
roots, we find the hunting people turning more
and more to such vegetable food as can be found in a
wild state; and as still more southern climates are
reached, agriculture appears and increases as we
go south, until it practically affords the sole means
of subsistence.   The wild foods were numerous;
berries and roots of all sorts are the staples in the
north, where lichens and the inner bark of certain
trees are also used.   In the Columbia Valley and
on the plateaus the root of the camass (*Camassia
esculenta*) is sought and obtained in great quantities,
and eaten either roasted or in cakes made from its

meal.   In central California the acorn is the great
source of food, and is likewise made into a meal
and subsequently prepared in various ways.   In the
southwest, besides the cultivated plants, the mesquite and the prickly-pear yield food; and in this
region mescal is generally eaten to produce a kind
of intoxication much in favor among the Indians.
In the northeast the wild - rice provision of the
Ojibwa has already been mentioned,[1] and wild
cranberries and the other small fruits of the Great
Lake region were also added to their diet.

East of the Mississippi and south of the St.
Lawrence basin, agriculture diminished the importance of wild fruits, but they still contributed to
the Indian's larder.   It is needless to specify in
detail, for it can truly be said that every edible
plant was made use of by the natives; and it was only
in certain regions where a given variety exerted a
marked influence on the residence, such as the
water-lily among the Klamath, the camass on the
plateaus, and the wild rice among the Ojibwa and
other eastern tribes, that it deserves especial mention.   Of cultivated plants, maize, beans, squashes, and tobacco must be accorded the first place,
particularly in the southeast.   In certain regions,
notably the southwest, these plants were supple-
mented by the seeds of the sunflower.

Of animal food, what might be termed the transition form consisted of insects, for in the dry regions

[1] See above, chap. x.

of the west numerous species such as the grasshopper and various larvæ are dried, pounded into a meal, and mixed with vegetable products. Snakes and reptiles of all kinds are also eaten, unless religious considerations compel abstinence, as happens in a number of groups. The larger mammals were very naturally the chief contributors to the animal supply in areas where they existed. The seal, walrus, and polar-bear, the various members of the deer family, bears, mountain-sheep, mountain-goat, antelope, and, above all, the bison, have been the mainstay of the tribes living in the same habitats as those animals. Small mammals of every sort are eaten everywhere, and the importance of fish in such regions as the north Pacific coast cannot be over-estimated.

The Indian methods of hunting were in general crude, except that much ingenuity was shown in devising traps for small mammals and for fish. With the bow and arrow and various spears and clubs as the chief weapons, success depended upon close range, and as a consequence stalking and driving were the ordinary means of approach to the larger land animals. Clever disguises of animal heads and skins were quite generally adopted to deceive the quarry in stalking. The advent of the horse gave a new method of hunting the buffalo, which was quickly seized upon by the tribes of the plains; and the introduction of fire - arms has of course revolutionized the hunting customs of the

Indians from one side of the continent to the other. The harpoons and spears in use by the Eskimo and tribes of the northwest coast for hunting whales and the other large sea mammals were particularly ingenious in the devices of detachable points and floats, which afforded safety to the hunters without diminishing the efficiency of the weapons.

In preparing the foods thus obtained, roasting and boiling were the common methods of cooking. Boiling was ordinarily done by dropping heated stones into vessels filled with water, the receptacles being of wood, basketry, or pottery, occasionally of stone. Smoking and drying as methods of preserving meat were practised widely. The best-known process of drying was the so-called "jerking," which consisted of cutting the flesh into long, thin strips, which were then thoroughly dried in the sun. Meat thus prepared would keep indefinitely, and was cooked as needed. The jerked meat was sometimes pounded up and mixed with fat, the result being known as "pemmican," and was much used in the north. In the northwest, among the salmon-fishing tribes, the fish are split and thoroughly dried and smoked, after which they are stored for later use. Salt was obtained from natural deposits or from springs, and was generally known in the west and as far east as the Ohio Valley.

Domesticated animals can be disregarded as a source of food supply in early days, since it is probable that the dog was the only animal which would come under that head in pre-Columbian times. Dogs were eaten by certain tribes, but their chief usefulness was in other lines. It is almost certain that the horses which play so important a part in the life of the plains Indians are the descendants of those introduced by the first Europeans; and the sheep and goats which now afford the Navajo his chief means of subsistence are known to have come from the Spaniards.

Cannibalism as a practice can hardly be said to have existed in North America, certainly not north of the Mexican border. In certain tribes there were ceremonials in which the rite of eating human flesh, or at least the pretence, formed a part; and it has been thought that this expressed a survival from days when the custom was general. It was probably nothing more than the symbolic acquisition of the victim's powers, and there is no evidence that it ever had other significance. In practically all cases it was an empty form.

As among all peoples, food taboos occur in bewildering variety, especially among the Eskimo, and hardly an Indian group can be found that does not practise some kind of abstinence for religious reasons. These taboos are sometimes temporary, but sometimes permanent; in the latter cases there is always a traditional or mythological basis which gives the custom the strength of a religious principle.

CHAPTER XV

INDIAN INDUSTRIAL LIFE AND WARFARE
(1500–1900)

THE Indian's acquaintance with metal was little more than accidental, and his smithery was usually a rude beating out into the desired shape, with designs applied by etching or hammering. In Mexico, as was noted in a previous chapter, the art of casting metals had been attained, but it was practically unknown in the northern parts of the continent. Copper and gold were most commonly used, as the two metals most adaptable to the primitive technique of the savage.

Thrown back upon stone and wood as the chief sources of raw material, it is not strange that there developed that infinite variety of weapons, tools, and vessels of those substances which archæological research has brought to light. Where stone and wood were ill adapted, bone, antler, shell, and other durable materials were made to do service in the arts.

For certain necessaries, however, neither stone, wood, nor horn will answer. Clothing must be provided, and some workable substance was called for as material for the various vessels and receptacles of every-day life. The solution of these difficulties was found in the arts of skin-dressing, pottery, and weaving, in all of which the Indian reached a high degree of perfection. The unevenness of the distribution of these arts is, however, most striking. The knowledge of skin-dressing was widely diffused, but pottery-making was entirely absent in many regions; and while weaving in some form was practically universal, the degree of skill in the textile art varied from area to area in an inexplicable manner.

For the preparation of skins the treatment of buffalo hides by the Indians of the plains may be taken as an example. As soon as removed, the skin was spread, stretched, and pegged to the ground, with the flesh side up, and thus exposed to the blazing sun it soon became dry and hard. The subsequent manipulation depended upon the end in view. For robes, the woman began to chip away the surface with an adze of flint or other hard material, so as to reduce the skin to uniform thickness as well as to render it more pliable. It was here that the chief care was necessary, in order not to cut through at any point and yet to produce the desired thinness. To facilitate the process and to render the skin as soft as possible, it was constantly smeared with a mixture of buffalo brains and fat, which was thoroughly rubbed in with a smooth stone. The final product was as pliable as cloth. For tipi coverings the hair was removed by soaking the hide in water mixed with wood-ashes or some other alkaline substance, and both sides were treated as described above. For making parfleches or packing-cases, the hide was taken green, the hair removed, and a piece of the desired size was stretched upon a form, where it dried in the proper shape; and the rawhide product was practically indestructible.

Among all tribes in whose neighborhood deer were found, the skins were dressed more or less as above, and the resulting buckskin was wonderfully soft and workable. From the far north to the extreme south this buckskin was the chief material used for clothing. The women of many tribes attained great skill in cutting and fitting, as well as in sewing the garments with sinew thread, which was the method universally practised. The typical man's clothing consisted of a breech-cloth, a hunting-shirt, leggings, and moccasins. The Indian woman wore a loose, short-sleeved upper garment, a waist-cloth or apron, leggings, and moccasins, the last two articles often being made in one piece. Young children usually went entirely naked. On the northwest coast, where the climate is wet and rainy, capes and aprons of woven cedar bark have been devised to meet the conditions. Among the Eskimo, where the climate necessitates the wearing of furs during a large part of the year, and where during the milder season the men are forced to be much in the water, a very efficient water-proof suit is made from the intestines of seals.

The costume mentioned above as typical had nearly as many modifications as there were tribes. In certain parts of the far west the Indians wore practically nothing, and in Mexico elaborate dresses of different woven fabrics were in use. There was also great variety and magnificence in the different ceremonial costumes where symbolism had full sway. With the advent of the European and his manufactures, the clothing of the Indians has been affected along with the rest of his culture. The bead-work ornamentation, which is now regarded as peculiarly Indian, is of course a modern growth, though the designs may follow ancient motives. Embroidery with porcupine quills, which is still practised extensively in certain groups, was probably the forerunner of this type of embellishment. In nearly all parts of the United States the native clothing has given place to that of the whites; and it is only in the ceremonial costumes, where religious conservatism makes itself felt, that the Indian dress can be expected to survive for any time.

Much has been written of the modes of hair-dressing, and the subject is worth mention. In the eastern states generally the men shaved the head, leaving a crest along the centre, with a long scalp-lock, which was braided and decorated with great care. The arrangement of the scalp-lock varied among different groups, but in one form or

another it was found over the greater part of the
United States except along the Pacific coast.   Most
of the plains tribes did not shave the head, but
wore the hair either braided or flowing, but always
with the scalp-lock in evidence.   The southwestern
Indians usually cut the hair straight across the forehead in front and at the shoulders behind.

The Indians were fond of bodily ornament both
permanent and temporary; of the permanent form
were the flattened heads and other deformations.
Tattooing was much more widely practised among
the western tribes than in the east, but it is impossible to say what may have determined its
presence or absence in a given group.   In the extreme northwest, where it was more elaborate than
elsewhere, the designs are often of a totemic or
other symbolic character.   In many regions, however, the marks are simple lines and dots and
evidently purely decorative in purpose.

Labrets, or studs of bone, ivory, and wood, were
worn in the lower lip by the Indians of the northwest coast, and the custom persists in an attenu-
ated form among the Eskimo at the mouth of the
Mackenzie River, by whom it was doubtless borrowed from Alaska.[1]   The septum of the nose was
pierced by some tribes, notably on the plateaus and
the Pacific coast, and pendants of various forms
were inserted.   Ear ornaments of one form or

---

[1] Dall, " On Masks, Labrets, and Certain Aboriginal Customs "
(Bureau of Ethnology, *Third Annual Report*).

another were worn nearly everywhere.   The varieties of necklaces, armlets, and ornaments of that type are innumerable: shell, bone, teeth, and claws being the materials most in favor.

Painting of the face and body was universal among the Indians, and was regarded as an indispensable adjunct to dress and adornment.   The original pigments before the coming of the whites were red and yellow ochre, powdered charcoal, different earths, and the juices of many roots and plants.   The two colors most in use were red and black.   The application varied with the tribe as well as the occasion—every ceremonial required its particular form of painting, and every important event in the life of the individual was marked in the same way.

An important branch of industrial art was pottery.   Durable, water-tight vessels are conveniences everywhere, and in some regions absolute necessities.   It was probably then in response to a pressing condition of the environment that the potter's art reached its height in the arid regions of the southwest.   The discovery of the process of pot-making was doubtless aided by the fact that in precisely that climate sun-dried clay would occur naturally and give the needed suggestion to the early inventor.   The ruder examples of pottery are vessels modelled roughly and quickly with the fingers.   Even the Eskimo had attained this knowledge, and mixed clay with blood and hair to form a primitive but serviceable lamp, which hardened quickly under its own heat. The crudely modelled type of pottery is found widely distributed in North America, though great areas of the north and west are destitute of even that.

Among the tribes of the eastern woodlands, the gulf coast, and the southwest, pottery was seen at its best, and we may take the ware of the Pueblo as the most perfect type. The Indians had discovered that unmixed clay was brittle, and had devised the remedy as well; the Pueblo woman almost invariably introduces sand and powdered potsherds into her raw material ; and even the pottery of the ancient mounds of the Mississippi drainage shows that the clay was tempered by mixture with mica, pulverized shells, and other ingredients.

Besides the simple modelling of the soft material, the commonest method of pottery making is by "coiling." The woman rolls out a long, slender fillet of clay varying in thickness according to the size of the vessel to be made. This strip is coiled on itself to form a disk and the bottom of the vessel. The edges are then curved upward and strip after strip added, each one slightly overlapping the one next beneath until the desired size is reached. The rough surface is then smoothed out with the fingers or an appropriate instrument. Where the vessel is to be decorated, a slip or wash of fine clay mixed with water is often applied. The potters' wheel had never been invented by any people of the Western Hemisphere.

The æsthetic value of Indian pottery is either in the form or the surface decoration. In the older examples from the mounds there appears to have been a tendency to model the vessels in imitation of natural forms—animals, men, and the like. In the southwest the artistic impulse finds its chief expression in the coloring and surface decoration, which latter is painted on and fixed by firing.

Of textile industries basketry and matting are not only the most primitive, they are also the most wide-spread. In the study of savage technique basketry has afforded the best basis-for comparisons, and the distribution of types of manufacture and designs in this particular art in North America is so striking that much has been learned regarding the cultural relations of the Indian tribes from whom collections of basketry have been made.[1] The uses of basketry cannot be enumerated. It appears in every phase of the Indian's life; and being, in one form or another, distributed over practically the whole of the continent, it may be regarded as one of the most significant objects of Indian industry.

Woven and coiled basketry are the two types of technique, the former built on a warp foundation and the latter on a basis of rods or splints. Woven basketry is seen in its simplest form among the

---

[1] For an exhaustive and excellent account of Indian basketry, see Mason, *Aboriginal American Basketry*.

tribes of the northeastern woodlands, where strips of some hardwood, of uniform width and thickness, are woven in a plain, checker-board pattern. As soon as the strips are varied in width and coloring the possible patterns are numerous and the beauty much increased. Such an advance is seen in the cedar - bark weaving of the north Pacific coast. The great variety in form and pattern which woven basketry presents in different parts of the country is brought about by the treatment of the warp and weft strands, as well as by the different materials and pigments employed.

Coiled basketry is produced by sewing over a rod foundation with some flexible material, each stitch interlocking with the one beneath. This type is essentially a western and southwestern production.

The art of weaving cotton and wool into cloth was also an Indian accomplishment. The looms were of a simple sort, but the product was often of remarkable fineness and beauty, as in the blankets of the Tlingit and Navajo and the cloths of Central and South America.

It has already been noted that the exigencies of the food quest called for frequent changes of residence on the part of the Indian, and the journeys thus undertaken were often of considerable length. Modes of travel and means of transportation, therefore, were not only a matter of concern to the Indian himself, but are of interest as an additional expression of his adaptation to his environment.

On land, the narrow trail worn by the travellers on foot and in single file was the line of communication from point to point; and south of the arctic the means of transporting goods was on the backs of men and women. The dog, as the only domesticated animal, gave some assistance. In the open country of the west he was harnessed to two trailing poles, and was thus able to drag loads of seventy-five to one hundred pounds; and when the horse arrived, the same device on a larger scale was employed and the process of moving greatly facilitated.

Innumerable inventions were in use to lighten the labor of the human pack-animal. Baskets and receptacles of every kind, frames of various shapes were employed, but, above all, there was the "tump-line," or carrying-strap, which passed around the forehead or chest and supported the burden on the back. Snow-shoes are in use from the Eskimo domain to the latitude of the northern states. The size of the shoe and the fineness of the mesh increase as the temperature rises and the snow becomes softer and less compact.

Among the Eskimo and certain tribes of the far north, where the snow is deep and lasts for many months of the year, sledges drawn by men and dogs are the means of transportation. The runners are of drift-wood or bone, and shod with walrus, ivory, or whalebone; and in order to make them glide still more smoothly, a thin coating of ice is allowed to form. The dog harness is simple but effective, and the thongs which draw the sledge are attached by a toggle which can readily be cast off.

Travel by water saves much time and energy, and as a consequence navigation is practised by every known people. The typical boat of the American Indian is undoubtedly the bark canoe, found at its best in the northeast, where the necessary materials are plentiful and the demand for a portable craft is greatest. This canoe is built of several pieces of bark stretched over a frame of ribs and sewn together, as well as rendered water-proof at the seams with pitch.

It is not known whether the Eskimo skin canoe is a derivation of the bark canoe or not, but it would seem plausible that he carried the notion with him from his more southern home, and met the difficulty of lack of bark by utilizing the skins, of which he had great plenty. The "umiak," or women's boat, among the Eskimo is a large, open affair, built somewhat on the lines of an Indian canoe, and is the craft which carries the women, children, and household effects whenever the sea is open. The "kayak," or hunting-canoe, which is strictly the man's type, is entirely covered with skin, except for the small opening where the paddler sits.

Another type of skin boat is the coracle, or "bull boat," made by certain tribes of the plains and mentioned in the chapter descriptive of that group.[1] It was constructed of a buffalo hide stretched over a

[1] See above, chap. ix.

frame-work of poles, and though a clumsy, unwieldy craft, was a great aid in ferrying the Indians across such wide streams as the Missouri.

The dugouts are characteristic of the northwest Pacific and southeast Atlantic coasts, but reached their highest development in the former region. While difficult for the uninitiated to manage, and of no use where portages are frequent, the Indian skilled in their navigation can handle them with surprising ease and quickness.

The universal means of propulsion is the paddle. Oars were probably known to the Eskimo alone of all American peoples, and the culture of that race is constantly under the suspicion of having been affected by contact with Europeans. Sails of woven cedar bark from five to ten feet square were in common use along the north Pacific coast, where sea navigation was common and the wind could be utilized to great advantage. These primitive sails seem to have been used only with fair winds, as there was no device for shifting them after they had once been set.

The great obstacles to inland canoe navigation, the portages, have been discussed in an earlier chapter.[1] We need only emphasize once more the great importance of the Indian carrying-places in marking out the lines along which communication took place between the tribes and subsequent population tended to flow.

[1] See above, chap. ii.

Of an importance second to none were the methods of obtaining fire.[1] The great use of fire is of course for cooking, but light and heat become conditions of necessity in certain climates, and we find the Eskimo with their lamps, the northwestern Indians with their torches of candle-fish, and the eastern tribes with their blazing pine-knots making an attempt at illumination; and wherever fuel permitted, the burning fire became the centre of family, clan, and tribal life.

The simplest device for fire-making is the well-known "fire-drill," which is a vertical wooden rod twirled in a horizontal piece of dry wood. The friction produces a fine dry-wood dust which presently ignites from the heat, and by gentle treatment the spark is transferred to some inflammable material held ready for the purpose. The common method of operation is to twirl the upright or "spindle" between the palms of the hands, while the horizontal piece or "hearth" is held firmly on the ground by the knee or foot. This invention is found everywhere in North America, and was used with great facility by all Indians. Improvement in the apparatus was made by certain tribes by winding a cord once or twice around the upright and pulling it back and forth, thus creating a rapid and even rotary motion which hastened the result.

[1] Hough, " Fire-Making Apparatus," U. S. National Museum, *Report*, 1888, pp. 531–588; *ibid.*, 1890, pp. 395–409; Mason, *Origins of Invention*, 84.

Both hands being needed to operate the cord, several devices were made to keep the upright in place and still permit the work to be done by one individual. The Eskimo method was to hold in the mouth a bone or ivory socket into which the upper end of the spindle fitted and which held it in place while allowing it to rotate freely. Another way out of the difficulty was to attach the cord to a curved stick like a bowstring and work this back and forth or up and down, both of which actions can be carried out with one hand, leaving the other free to hold the spindle in position. The former of these methods is known as the bow - drill, the latter as the pump-drill. Both devices were used for boring holes in different materials by simply placing a hard, sharp point on the spindle. The pump is specifically a southwestern contrivance, though it has been reported among Indians of the east.

Fire-making by "ploughing" was also practised by some tribes, and consists in running the upright rapidly back and forth in a groove of its own making, and producing a dust which is then treated in exactly the same way as in the case of the drill. The Eskimo and northern Indians had also discovered that sparks and fire could be obtained by percussion, and made use of two pieces of pyrites, or of pyrites and flint, in exactly the same way that civilized man formerly operated with flint and steel.

The organization and distribution of the Indians

resulted in a continual state of war. Every tribe
was practically at war with every other with which
there was not an express treaty of peace. It is not
strange then that the military virtues came to hold
the highest place in the popular regard. To die in
battle was glorious; bravery, strength, and skill gave
the most envied positions to their possessors, and
cowardice was everywhere execrated. It was an
easy matter to arouse the warlike enthusiasm of the
boy, and among most tribes his early training was
directed chiefly to that end. The child's toys were
miniature weapons, and the games were usually
contests which practised the boys in their use.

The most widely distributed implements of war
were the bow and arrow, and were found everywhere.
The bow was made of the toughest, most elastic
wood to be found in the vicinity of the maker, and
in a few places a capable substitute was found in
horn. In the extreme north, where growing wood
was scarce, drift-wood was utilized and strengthened
by a backing of sinew. The use of sinew as a
reinforcement was seen at its best among the
northwestern tribes, where it was shredded out and
applied by means of fish or other animal glue, with
such skill that the union with the wood appears
complete. The length and form of the bow varied
with the locality. It was usually short, however,
not much over three feet as a rule. Bows manufactured from the horns of buffalo and mountain-
sheep were occasionally used by tribes of the plains

and the plateaus.   The ordinary bowstring was of sinew, twisted and braided to a point of great strength.

As much care and attention were given to the arrow as to the bow.   The shaft was of hard wood or cane, the point of stone, flint, obsidian, or jasper (in more modern days of iron or glass), and the arrow was tipped with eagle feathers.   Poison was sometimes applied to the points.

The hatchet or tomahawk was a characteristic weapon of the Indians, except in the far north, and was especially in favor in the east, where the forest made hand - to - hand fighting a constant necessity.   The tomahawk came to be used as a symbol of war, and in many tribes was constructed so as to form a pipe as well, and as such was employed in many ceremonies.

Short lances or javelins were used in Mexico and on the Pacfic coast, as well as by the Eskimo. Their efficiency was increased by the "throwing stick," which gave a much longer range than could be reached by hand.   War-clubs were used everywhere, and knives or short cutting weapons of various sorts were also universal.

Thrusting-lances or spears were apparently not common, though they were used extensively by the tribes of the plains, whose battles were waged on horseback.   These Indians also made use of shields, light but tough affairs of rawhide, which were mainly for parrying the opponent's lance.   Much attention was given to the decoration of these shields, the designs being symbolic and of a deep religious significance to the owners. Other defensive armor was practically confined to the Pacific coast and the plateaus, where a cuirass of wooden slats or sticks was the means of protection. Thick hide was also used in some places.

Military art can hardly be said to have existed. Besides the natural advantages of land formations, fortifications consisted only of stockades, or occasionally of a rampart of earth reinforced by a ditch. Campaigns were little more than sudden raids carried out by small bodies of warriors brought together for the particular occasion. Surprises and ambuscades were the limit of the Indian devices. Massacre without mercy was the rule, though prisoners were sometimes taken, and either put to death at some later time or adopted into the tribe of the captors, or made slaves, as the case might be. Adoption following capture was much more common among the tribes of the eastern woodlands than in other parts of the continent; and slavery, as has been shown, was more prevalent in the extreme west than elsewhere.

Torture of prisoners was also more common in the east, but even there was not as general as is popularly supposed. Selected individuals were taken for the purpose, and there was usually a religious motive behind the practice. It was also a custom in many tribes to eat the flesh of one of the victims after a victory. This was done with the idea of assimilating the powers and desirable qualities of the slain, and was as far as the practice of cannibalism ever went.

Scalping was a custom over the whole continent north of Mexico, except at certain points on the Pacific slope and among the Eskimo. The chief value of the scalp was as a trophy and proof of the warrior's prowess, though there was also, probably, a deeper reason behind the custom. The possession of the scalp may have signified a certain power over the soul of the victim, in a way analogous to similar customs in other parts of the world. Scalps were variously worn and displayed by the takers, and often figured in religious ceremonials.

Among many Indians, notably in the middle west, a warrior's reputation rested upon the number of "*coups*" which stood to his credit in the records of the tribe. A *coup* was a deed of special prowess, and the particular acts which enabled a man to count *coup* were definitely laid down and universally recognized. The most usual acts which carried the privilege were killing and scalping an enemy, being the first to touch an enemy in an attack, rescuing a wounded fellow, and stealing a horse from the enemy's camp.

The organization of a campaign was usually informal in its beginning. An individual would announce his intention to conduct a raid and ask for volunteers to accompany him. His success in mustering a band would naturally depend upon his reputation as a warrior and his powers of persuasion. It must be remembered that all military service was everywhere voluntary, the only force compelling an unwilling man to join a war-party being public opinion and the dread of being considered a coward. Among the more highly organized tribes and confederacies extensive campaigns for purposes of defence were decided upon by the tribal or confederation council, and the execution of the decision was left to the recognized war-chief or chiefs, but even in such cases the service of the individual was voluntary. Occasionally war would be declared with considerable formality, and notice sent by means of belts or symbolic objects, and treaties of peace were made and sealed in the same way. The authority of the leader was vague, though usually recognized while the campaign was in progress. Punishment for disobedience was seldom anything more than expulsion from the band and ridicule at the hands of the women and children upon the culprit's return home.

Before leaving on the war-path a dance was participated in by the intending warriors, the obvious purpose being to inflame their passion and increase their enthusiasm; and upon the return from a successful raid, dances and ceremonies of celebration and thanksgiving were held, and often developed into the wildest orgies.

While the wars of the Indians among themselves

were constant they were usually on a small scale. Nevertheless, the formation of confederacies brought about a condition which united large bodies of men, and sometimes produced active hostilities of such magnitude and duration that they exerted a profound influence on the distribution of the tribes Such, for example, was the effect of the Iroquois League, whose struggle with surrounding Algonquian tribes lasted for centuries and determined the native occupancy of the entire northeastern portion of the United States. The same was true of the Creek confederacy in the southeast; while the Cherokee were strong enough in themselves to form a barrier to all encroachment. The Sioux or Dakota confederacy was the dominant power in the middle west and completely controlled the northern portions of the great plains. The tribes of the Pacific slope were more sedentary and less warlike than those of the east, and their wars were probably always of a petty sort. In the south the Aztec confederacy conducted elaborate campaigns and held permanent sway.

It is quite evident that the two chief incentives to war among the Indians were defence and revenge. Disputes regarding the indefinite territory between recognized tribal limits were also a fruitful cause of hostilities, the Indian violently resenting any encroachment upon what he regarded as his own province. Offensive campaigns were sometimes undertaken as preventive measures to anticipate

attacks and to inspire fear, and thus to insure freedom from outside interference.   Whatever the ex-
citing cause of actual hostilities, when once begun
it was difficult to bring them to a close.   The
universal law of blood revenge demanded satisfaction for every death, and a retaliatory act simply
shifted the side of the obligation, so that, unless
an understanding was reached, the only outcome
was mutual extinction.   This principle undoubtedly
lay at the root of much of the Indian warfare.

With the coming of the whites the entire aspect
changed.   The common enemy encouraged intertribal alliances before undreamed of, as was shown
in many of the early struggles between the colonists
and the Indians in New England and other parts of
the east.   Rapid and violent shiftings of location
were also necessitated by the new pressure, and
these met determined resistance from the occupants
of the territory which was thus invaded.   Coalitions
with the whites were sought as a means of successfully dealing with Indian enemies, and the more
effective weapons thus obtained added to the de-
structiveness of the wars.   The history of the Indian
tribes since the arrival of Europeans is the history
of constant struggle, movement, and change, and
still remains to be written.

CHAPTER XVI

INDIAN RELIGION, MYTHOLOGY, AND ART

(1500–1900)

IT has come to be generally recognized that the universal characteristic of religion in its more primitive expression is a belief in spirits. The conceptions which underlie the beliefs are usually crude but none the less distinct. This animism, to use the convenient term now commonly employed,[1] is variously expressed in beliefs and consequent rites and ceremonies. Among the American Indians, who are no exception to the rule, the animistic conception includes all nature. Every individual, every animal, every object, every concrete phenomenon has its soul or spirit. In the case of men and lower animals these souls are regarded as existing after the death of the body, and hence there has arisen a vast collection of souls or spirits without bodies, which take an interest in worldly affairs and are capable of interfering to the advantage or detriment of mankind. The supplication and propitiation of these spirits in their various forms and functions constitute the religious ceremonials of the Indian.

[1] Cf. Tylor, *Primitive Culture*, I., 425

There is a difficulty in analyzing the beliefs which underlie such outward manifestations, because the religion of the Indian is interwoven with every other phase of his life. ˙ It is impossible, for example, to disentangle the religious from the social aspect of totemism, or the religious from the æsthetic in art. The two sets of ideas are in every case inevitably and inextricably associated and the exact delimitation of either is impossible.

To the mind of the Indian anything which was strange was "mystery," and to "mystery" was referred in all the languages, everything incomprehensible. This is the meaning of the word "manitou," of Algonquian origin, now so widely used for corresponding conceptions throughout the tribes of the continent. Primarily an adjective, it has come to be employed as a noun, and spirits are called "manitous" as personifications of this quality. As a matter of course, some of these spirits are more powerful than others, and there are, therefore, grades of manitous, and sometimes one in particular, who will be venerated or feared more than any other. There is not, however, any conception of an all-powerful deity or "great spirit."

It was the misapprehension of the character of the manitou by the early missionaries and observers, and their tendency to read their own ideas into the Indian religions, that gave rise to the error. The particular manitou which would hold the first place in any given group was naturally determined by the general mode of life. Among the plains Indians the spirit of the buffalo was the one to be considered above all others; while among other tribes the sun, rain, spirits of various crops, etc., were the powers to be propitiated. In the cult of these great or class manitous the tribal rites and ceremonies developed, reaching the elaboration already described in preceding chapters. They were characterized by dancing and symbolic dramatic performances of great complexity, often lasting for weeks. Hysterical manifestations of all sorts were usual and the excitement was often intense. Intoxicants and narcotics were employed to aid in the production of the nervous state, which was regarded as indispensable for intimate association with the spirits. These dances were usually invocations for abundant harvests, for rain, for success in hunting or war, or were festivals of thanksgiving for favors already bestowed. In the more highly developed of the ceremonials the custom of sacrifice had been introduced, reaching in Mexico a point where human beings were made the victims.

The religious customs relating to death and burial form a class by themselves, but are based upon the same animistic ideas which underlie all the religious beliefs. The soul of the dead man was believed to exist after death and to have needs similar to those of the body in life; consequently, offerings of all sorts were made at the grave, which could be utilized by the soul in its spirit life. A curious conception of a multiplicity of soul was also present in some of the tribes. Each individual was believed to be animated by several spirits which had different functions after death. One, for example, would remain near the body, one would haunt the village, one would go to the land of the dead, the so-called "happy hunting-grounds," etc.

Methods of burial were many and various. Graves, stone - pits or cists, caves, or huts were used by many tribes. Mummification was practised in some regions, and cremation was also employed by certain groups. ⸌An interesting mode in fairly common use was the disposal of the corpse in a tree or on a scaffold, and in some cases the body was exposed to be devoured by beasts and birds. No matter what the method might be, it was carried out with rigid ceremony and the most religious care.

One of the most important practices, if not the fundamental religious custom of the Indian, was the acquisition of a personal protecting spirit or manitou by the individual.[1] The details of the methods by which this supernatural helper was obtained varied from tribe to tribe, but the essential features remained the same. The individual who thus put himself in an especially close relation with a spirit became a shaman or medicine-man, and the more powerful his protecting manitou the more powerful was the shaman. Among certain tribes, as in the northwest, almost any one could, with per-

[1] See above, chap. viii.

sistence, acquire one of these guardian spirits: while
in other regions comparatively few were favored,
and the successful ones were proportionally feared
and respected.

In this communication with the spirits the shaman
obtained by practice and piety great influence over
them, and was therefore the person called in to ex-
pel a spirit of illness from an invalid or to conduct
a ceremony of wider import.   The procedure in the
cure of sickness was much the same in all parts of
the continent.   The shaman danced and sang his
particular songs, performed various manipulations
of a special and symbolic character, and thus forced
the spirit of the disease to leave the body of the
sick person.   The successes were surprisingly numerous, for the Indian is markedly hysterical in
temperament, and suggestion has in him a most
favorable soil on which to operate.   Failures were
easily explained by the counter influences of hostile
spirits or shamans.   A few striking cures would of
course add to the effectiveness of all future suggestive treatments, and particular shamans in this way
gained reputations which spread far beyond the
borders of their own tribes.

In most of these cases the shaman was guided
and assisted by his own particular supernatural
helper.   Some shamans would acquire more than
one guardian, and with time would come to stand
in a particularly close relation with the spirit world
in general.   They would then possess rather the

character of priests, though the essentials of their equipment were still strictly those of the primitive shaman or sorcerer. In the carrying out of elaborate ceremonies, like those of the southwest, organization was necessary, and there arose shamanistic societies or brotherhoods which gained great power and influence. These societies were often secret in character, which increased their popular prestige.

The character of the chief ceremonials of the Indians has been referred to in the various descriptive chapters. The most elaborate of these ceremonies are in the southwest, and it is possible to trace a gradual modification from that region as a base. Passing north over the great plains the importance and complexity of the religious rites are still great, but become progressively less, until the elaborate ceremonies disappear in the forests of the north. Tracing the characteristics eastward along the gulf coast we find the green-corn dance playing an all important rôle in the lives of the southeastern tribes, but its complexity is not to be compared with that of similar ceremonies in the Pueblo region, and it decreases as the northern tribes are reached.

Northwest from the Pueblo the plateau tribes exhibit little that even remotely suggests the ceremonies of the southwest; and in California a simple type also exists, though more intricate than on the plateaus. A certain amount of contact be-

tween California and the southwest is undeniable.
The north Pacific coast has its distinctive religious
rites, just as it is peculiar in its other phases of
culture. The underlying ideas are not, however,
essentially different from those of the rest of the
continent. There is, then, a progressive simplifica-
tion northward, but whether the process has been
one of degeneration in that direction or of elaboration in the other it is impossible to say. The
sun-dance and similar rites of the plains, and the
green - corn dance of the southeast, give the impression of degeneration; but beyond that there is
little to indicate the direction of development.

Certain religious movements of a relatively new
character occur from time to time and demonstrate the extreme suggestibility of the Indian,
which has been mentioned above. These upheavals
usually follow the appearance of a prophet, and
often spread over vast areas and include diverse
stocks. The ghost-dance religion, which has swept
the west in recent years, is a good example of such
movements. They are usually characterized by a
Messianic idea which is especially strong in Indian
tradition.

The mythology of the Indians is voluminous and
interesting. It is also important as affording the
most available means of tracing contact and intercommunication between tribes and stocks. The most
wide-spread and characteristic myths are those relating to the genesis of the tribes and their trans-

formation from an early condition of misfortune
and misery to a better state.　Creation myths as
such can hardly be said to exist, though in California
and a few other regions stories are told which
might properly come under that term.　The usual
genesis myth is of a period when the earth was
wholly different from what it is now.　People existed then, but not in their present form.　There
was no particular differentiation between men and
animals.　People were ignorant, poor, and miserable,
and the world was harried by monsters with which
the people could not cope.　There was no daylight
and no fire and no knowledge of the arts.　It was a
period pre-eminently of mystery and magic.

In this world of mystery appears the transformer or wanderer or culture hero, as he is variously
termed, who travels about working wonders, chang-
ing the existing order of things, and bringing affairs
more or less into the condition in which they are at
present.　The account of the transformer's journeys,
adventures, and achievements is the typical Indian
myth, and usually forms a cycle about which the
other stories cluster.　There is usually an introduction treating of the birth and early life of the
transformer, and this is followed by the history of his
deeds, which forms the main part of the myth.
After his work is ended the transformer disappears
in a miraculous manner, or is turned into stone, or
terminates his career in some extraordinary way.
His return is confidently expected by the Indians,

and it is this Messianic doctrine which gives the numerous Indian prophets their main hold and influence. In many tribes there are several transformers, who appear successively but whose functions are similar.

It is this being who is the great hero of the Indians and who was the great spirit or manitou to whom the early writers so frequently refer. A puzzling incongruity in his character is the fact that he is almost invariably a trickster and one who gains his ends by petty and despicable means. While usually triumphant in his various encounters, he is nevertheless often worsted or made ridiculous. In short, he is not at all the venerable personage one might expect.

Two explanations have been offered to account for this psychological incongruity, neither of which is sufficient. One holds that the buffoonery and trickery are late introductions and that the present myths are in a state of degeneration from a higher and purer form;[1] and the other that the transformer devises the arts and obtains the benefits for his own ends, to assist him in his own difficulties, and that man is only incidentally the beneficiary; and that the Indian feels himself under no obligation to venerate the transformer, since the latter had no altruistic purpose in mind.[2] With regard to the

[1] Brinton, *Myths of the New World.*
[2] Boas, in introduction to Teit, *Thompson River Indian Traditions.*

first theory, that of degeneration, there is not the slightest evidence of such a lowering in the majority of the myths; and in reply to the last it may be said that in many, if not most, of the transformer stories the hero does bestow his favors for the express benefit of mankind, and for no other apparent reason. In other words, the incongruity still remains a problem.

An immense number of stories are also told which usually have to do with the animals in the days when they lived and acted like men; and these myths supplement the transformer cycles in the explanation of present conditions. Natural phenomena, social institutions, customs and ceremonies of all sorts are thus accounted for, and in the rehearsal of the myths the children were instructed and trained in the rules and duties which awaited them as adult members of society. Many of the elements in these myths can be traced from tribe to tribe for immense distances, some stories being found in practically every corner of North America. Some of these coincidences may doubtless be accounted for by independent growth under the influence of similar psychological conditions; but in other cases dissemination from a common source is the only reasonable explanation.

It is to be expected that the æsthetic expression of the Indian will vary with the environment, and that different types of art will develop in different areas. In decorative art it is natural that a pottery-making group, for example, should possess a type of decoration and design sharply differentiated from that in use where pottery is unknown. There is nevertheless a wide distribution of certain types of design which requires notice.

Primitive art in general serves a useful as well as a strictly æsthetic end, and the fact that ornamentation, apparently purely decorative, often has a significance of another sort is now universally recognized. The development of geometrically symmetrical patterns from pictorial designs has been much discussed in recent years, and the art of the American Indian is a good example of the process. In many cases the realistic element in the patterns is no longer traceable, while the design yet carries a meaning easily recognized by the native. This symbolic character of Indian art is its most striking feature. In many cases the symbolism is undoubtedly read into the design, while in others it has developed through a gradual course of conventionalization.

The art of the west is much richer than that of the east, and it is on the north Pacific coast, the plains, and in the southwest that we find the most considerable æsthetic development. The northwest coast art is unique. It exhibits itself both in carving and in painting, as well as, to some extent, in weaving. In this region realism is never entirely lost sight of, and in the portrayal of animals, which form their motives, a certain resemblance is always discernible. Conventional modifications have naturally arisen, and strict rules which the artist may not transgress in his creation seem to have been developed. In a word, the aim of the north Pacific decoration seems to be to portray as much of the pattern animal as possible; and in order to accomplish this, the method employed is such dissection and distribution of the parts as may be necessary.

South of Vancouver Island and east of the coast mountains the type of decorative art changes completely. New motives are introduced and geometrical designs are substituted for the type just described. On the plateaus and in California basketry is the chief vehicle of decoration, and plants, artificial objects, and geographical features offer most of the suggestions for designs. The decorative art of the eastern tribes was meagre, and practically nothing is known of its significance.

On the plains the decorative impulse expends itself mainly on the rawhide parfleches and in bead - work, the designs in both fields having a symbolic and often intricate character. The point of interest here is the variation in method of interpretation of designs of the same general type. In each group the symbolism seems to be determined by the mental character of the people, and we find religious, military, hunting, or industrial interpretations as the case may be. In the southwest the opportunities are more numerous, pottery, basketry, and blankets offering a field for artistic creation which has produced a rich variety in expression. Little is known of the meanings of these patterns, but the symbolism is probably mainly religious.

In the personal decorations used in dances and ceremonials of all sorts much ingenuity is displayed, and as these performances are for the most part dramatic in character the dress and decoration usually indicate a particular mythological being whom the actor is impersonating. In this way has grown up the use of the grotesque masks of the northwest and the bizarre decorations and disguises of the plains and the southwest.

The most immediate expression of æsthetic impulse is probably the dance, and the passion with which primitive peoples indulge in this form of excitement is well known. The variety of Indian dances is of course very great and they cannot be described in detail. The influence of the dance, however, in bringing a group of individuals under the sway of a single emotion with their energies directed towards a single end, as in the war-dance, and its consequent importance as a social factor, can easily be imagined.

Indian music is distinguished by rhythm, often extremely complex, rather than by melody. Instrumental music is little more than the beating of time in accompaniment to the songs. The ritualistic songs are usually long chants or recitatives rehearsing the traditions or myths connected with the particular ceremony. Songs of war, love, ridicule, and those which accompany gambling and the incantations of shamans are the main forms besides the religious chants.   Musical instruments are limited to drums of various sorts, whistles, and rattles.

It is evident from the preceding survey of Indian sociology, religion, and art that these three aspects of their life are always interwoven.   It is impossible to interpret the expressions of any one of them except in the light of the others.   While this close association of divergent classes of ideas is characteristic of lower levels of culture in all parts of the world, it comes out with exceptional clearness in North America, and is the most striking characteristic of Indian psychology.

CHAPTER XVII

CHARACTER AND FUTURE OF THE INDIANS
(1904)

THE most striking facts with regard to the American Indian are his physical uniformity and his cultural diversity. In physical type the differences which characterize the tribes are slight, when compared with the common features of the natives of both North and South America. The causes of such physical variations as do appear must be sought in the causes of zoological variation everywhere, and it is impossible to come to a conclusion as to the exact and immediate influences.

Environment and mode of life, moreover, so affect physical types that when a general truth seems to emerge, a contradictory fact is sure to be forthcoming. The Eskimo of the arctic are usually cited, for example, as proofs of the stunting effects of excessively rigorous climate and life, and it is certainly true that as a rule they are undersized; but the Eskimo of the Mackenzie region are tall, active, and muscular, and remain so under exactly the same conditions as their shorter relatives, a local trait which may be of as much significance

as the more general feature.   It can hardly be a
mere accident, however, that the tribes of the northwest coast are short and heavily built, while the
Indians of the plains are tall and lithe.   The sea-
faring life of the former, which is spent mainly in
canoes, and the active hunting and, in modern days,
equestrian habits of the latter have undoubtedly
contributed to the selection of the physique.   The
shape and dimensions of the skull, which are studied
with great assiduity by anthropologists, indicate
nothing striking with regard to the Indian;[1] he is
ordinarily of the mesocephalic type, though exhibiting extremes of long-headedness and broad-
headedness in special instances.

Skull measurements are chiefly interesting as
giving some information with respect to the brain
within, and capacity is therefore of more significance
than shape.   The possible discrepancy, however, between the size of the skull and that of the brain it
contains is so great that examination of the brain
itself is the only safe basis for conclusions.   It is,
therefore, unfortunate that thus far there is not a
single authentic record of a North American Indian brain ever having been scientifically examined.
The indications from skull measurements would
be that the Indian brain is, on the average, slightly
smaller than that of the European, but any inferences with regard to consequent mental inferiority
are unsafe.   As a matter of fact, the evidence in

[1] See above, chap. x.

the psychological field tends to show that such mental differences as occur are due to experience and environment rather than to innate differences of mental capacity.[1]

The common statement and popular belief that the Indian has senses more acute than the white man has been shown to mean nothing more than that the Indian is trained in certain fields of observation, for wherever the European is practised under the same conditions he acquires the same skill as the native. The usual belief that Indian ethics and art are lower than those of the whites carries us no further, for in conformity to the standards which he recognizes, the Indian compares favorably with his white competitor. The few cases which have occurred in which an Indian has been entirely removed from his natural environment at an early age and educated amid civilized surroundings seem to show no particular inferiority in mental capacity.

Whatever the truth with respect to innate ability, tradition and social environment are the determining forces in the expression of Indian character as in that of all other races. It is hard to understand the numerous misconceptions in even the educated mind with regard to Indian character and habits. Probably the commonest conception of the Indian is of a grave, gloomy, taciturn, and

[1] Boas, " The Mind of Primitive Man " (*Science*, N. S., XIII., 281).

sullen individual. On the contrary, he is in his ordinary life a cheerful, talkative, gossipy person, with a great fondness for society. It is a matter of Indian training and social convention to be dignified and deliberate on all occasions of a public character, and as meetings with whites have most frequently been of that nature, the popular error arose, and persists in spite of the abundant testimony to the contrary from competent observers.

The stoicism with respect to pain which has been celebrated for centuries was simply another example of this conventional training. In his home life the Indian often exhibits the most childish behavior over physical pain, while he would submit to public torture without a moan. In his nervous make-up he is very hysterical, and the suggestive phenomena of religious excitements as witnessed in Indian gatherings are the counterparts of those seen on similar occasions among the negroes and certain elements of our own white population.

It has already been remarked that this suggestibility is the secret of the success and influence of the medicine - man, or shaman.[1] It also explains the presence of many disorders admirably adapted to suggestive treatment. Many observers have remarked the ease with which the Indian succumbs to disease and misfortune, and the hysterical temperament is undoubtedly the chief factor in this weakness.

[1] See above, chap. xvi.

The lack of immunity against infectious and epidemic diseases must be laid to a different source. These come from the whites, and the Indians have not yet acquired the racial immunity. As a consequence, measles, scarlet - fever, and small - pox have a mortality among the aborigines which greatly exceeds that among the whites—a single epidemic of measles will sometimes almost extinguish an Indian village or tribe. Whether or not epidemic diseases of any sort existed before the coming of the Europeans is doubtful. At the present time tuberculosis is creating havoc on many of the reservations, particularly on the Pacific slope, where the wet climate creates conditions favorable for its progress. In some tribes tuberculosis is so prevalent that practically every individual shows evidence of it. Syphilis and other venereal diseases also contribute to the deterioration of many stocks.

Another Indian trait which has been widely noted is hospitality. This was undoubtedly the outcome of the communal life where property was common and individual ownership hardly existed. The term is, therefore, somewhat misapplied, since food was regarded as free, and the individual owner nothing more than a custodian by force of circumstance.

The misconception with regard to the position of woman has also been noticed. In tribes where the matriarchate was fundamental, as among the

Iroquois, it is not strange that the woman should have demanded and received thorough recognition and respect; but it is noteworthy that in loosely organized tribes, where the clan does not obtain, and where the will of the stronger male might be expected to operate as the only law, she also asserts her rights with success. The applause of the women is often as much sought as the approval of the men, and an individual's social position can easily be made quite untenable by the opposition of the weaker sex. In general the highest ambition of the Indian is social regard and rank; and ridicule and ostracism are correspondingly feared and avoided. It was this sensitiveness to public opinion which enabled the tribal and other councils to remain as successful instruments of government without the establishment of a recognized executive.

These popular misconceptions are not merely of academic interest. They have played an important part in the chapter of American history which covers the relations of the white man and his government towards the Indians. Leaving entirely out of account the dishonesty and oppression which have been too frequent in the administration of Indian affairs, the failure to understand and appreciate the workings of the Indian mind and the nature of many of his customs, has led to well-intended interference, which has often produced serious disturbance, unrest, and revolt. Such, for example, has been the history of the attempts of the United

States to establish the ownership and succession of Indian lands. To impose a system of male inheritance upon a group accustomed to reckoning descent through the mother is not only incomprehensible but revolutionary, and inevitably meets with the stoutest resistance except from those who may be thereby unexpectedly benefited. The ownership of land in severalty is an idea repugnant as it is novel to many tribes, and, as experience has shown, is requiring generations of cautious management to bring about.

Much undeserved censure has been imposed upon the Indian department of the government by enthusiastic but badly informed friends of the aborigines. The difficulties of administration are enormous and are naturally not lessened by ignorance. Probably the most serious error, as it is the most difficult to avoid, is legislation for a heterogeneous population as if it were a homogeneous group. To apply the same rules and regulations to the Sioux as to the Zuñi is as inadvisable as it is in practice impossible. Even the same stocks exhibit such wide differentiations in culture that linguistic relationship cannot be used to mark the limits of uniform groups for purposes of administration. When a family like the Shoshonean can exhibit such extremes as the degraded bands commonly known as "Digger Indians," and a people capable of such heights of development as the Aztec of Mexico, all principles of classification must give way to that of progress in culture, in devising means of dealing with the Indian problem of the day.

The reservation method of handling the Indians was probably the only feasible one, but it has entirely changed the distribution of linguistic families. The disturbance has been much more marked in the east, where white immigration quickly crowded the territory, than in the west, where the Indians could be allowed to remain at least in the general neighborhood of their former seats. Most of the southeastern tribes were transferred bodily to Indian Territory, though in some cases small reservations were established near their old homes. In the west, reservations were formed at many different points; and are being kept up as far as Indian necessity demands and political pressure will permit.

Of the Algonquian group, most of the eastern tribes have disappeared entirely. The Canadian tribes of this family have not suffered as did the representatives in the United States, and still remain fairly numerous. The great Ojibwa division has bands both in Canada and in several of the northern states of the middle west. The western representatives, the Blackfeet, Arapaho, and Cheyenne, are all on western reservations or in Indian Territory and Oklahoma. The remnants of the eastern and the central Algonquians are, for the most part, in the last-named territories.

The Iroquoians, with the exception of the Cherokee, are divided between the United States and Canada.

They have all adapted themselves measurably to
the methods of civilized life.   Reservations for some
of the Six Nations were established in New York
state, and are still kept up, while the remainder
of the tribes are in Ontario, Wisconsin, and Indian
Territory.   The Cherokee, with the representatives
of the Muskhogean family, the Creek, Choctaw,
Chickasaw, and Seminole, make up the so-called
civilized tribes in Indian Territory, and are all self-
supporting and prosperous.

The Siouan family occupies numerous reservations in Wisconsin, Minnesota, North and South
Dakota, Montana, Nebraska, Kansas, and Indian
Territory, with a considerable number in Canada;
they do not exhibit great adaptability to civilized
life.   The Athapascan Indians have remained comparatively untouched in the far north; while the
southern representatives, the Apache and Navajo,
in Arizona, New Mexico, and Mexico, have been
much in contact with Europeans.   The Navajo are
self-supporting and prosperous, but the Apache are
still primitive in life, though of late years peace-
ful enough in disposition.   The Shoshonean tribes
are distributed on reservations in Idaho, Utah,
Nevada, California, and Arizona, with the Comanche
in Indian Territory.   The Pawnee are mainly in
Indian Territory.   The Pacific coast tribes, nearly
all small and rapidly diminishing, are on numerous
small reservations, usually near their original habitats.

The future of the Indians cannot be predicted with confidence. It has been shown that while decreasing in numbers, the diminution is not rapid.[1] It is quite conceivable, even if not probable, that more thorough adaptation to a civilized environment might check the process of extinction and place the birth-rate higher than the death-rate. Absorption by the whites is regarded by many as the natural and ultimate outcome; and the increasing number of mixed bloods on the reservations indicates such a possibility. The product of such mixture seems also to be well adapted to survive. There is no evidence that the often described undesirable qualities of the mixed blood are inherent in the crossing, but in most cases they are traits fostered by the unfortunate social environment in which such an individual finds himself. Virtually an outcast from both the higher and lower groups, it is not strange that the adult halfbreed should exhibit questionable characteristics. The half-blood woman is also more prolific than the full-blood, which is a point of great significance in forecasting the future. In the light of the processes now in operation, gradual absorption by the surrounding whites seems to be the Indian's most probable fate.

[1] See above, chap. vi.

CHAPTER XVIII

CRITICAL ESSAY ON AUTHORITIES

PHYSIOGRAPHY

THERE are several trustworthy works describing the general physical features of North America. J. D. Whitney, *The United States* (1889), published in part in the ninth edition of the *Encyclopædia Britannica*, is a comprehensive, authoritative account of the physical geography and material resources of that portion of the continent. N. S. Shaler, *United States of America* (2 vols., 1897), by various authors, considers the economic development of the nation in relation to the natural resources, and will be found useful. Shaler's chapter on " Physiography of North America," in Justin Winsor, *Narrative and Critical History of America*, IV. (1884), is also good. The chapters on "North America" and "The United States," by W. M. Davis, in Mill, *International Geography* (1900), are admirable condensed descriptions, and emphasize the relation of the physical features to the growth of population. J. B. Tyrrell's chapter on the "Dominion of Canada" in the same work is along the same lines. Most of the modern encyclopædias also contain well-digested general accounts. On the subject of drainage, Israel Russell, *Rivers of North America* (1898), may be relied upon. The reports of the geological and other surveys of the United States government and of the several

states are the great sources of information on special
physiographic topics.

WATERWAYS, PORTAGES, TRAILS, AND MOUNTAIN-PASSES

On the general subject of the effect of geographical
conditions on exploration and settlement in North America
there are two books: E. C. Semple, *American History and
Its Geographic Conditions* (1903), and A. P. Brigham,
Geographic Influences in American History (1903). They
are both good, the former emphasizing tne historical stand-
point and the latter the geographical.   F. Ratzel, *Politische
Geographie der Vereinigten Staaten von America* (1903),
should also be consulted.   Archer Butler Hulbert, *Historic
Highways of America* (11 vols., 1902–1904), offers much
interesting information of a somewhat sketchy character
regarding early routes of travel.   The volumes thus far
published are: I. *Paths of the Mound-Building Indians and
Great Game Animals* (1902), II. *Indian Thoroughfares*
(1902), III. *Washington's Road (Nemacolin's Path)* (1903),
IV. *Braddock's Road* (1903), V. *The Old Glade (Forbes's)
Road* (1903), VI. *Boone's Wilderness Road* (1903), VII.
Portage Paths (1903), VIII. *Military Roads of the Mississippi
Basin* (1904), IX. *Waterways and Western Expansion*
(1903), X. *The Cumberland Road* (1904), XI. *Pioneer
Roads and Experiences of Travellers* (1904).   The accounts
of the early travellers and traders are the sources of information regarding the routes of the north and northwest.
Alexander Mackenzie, *Voyages from Montreal to the Frozen
and Pacific Oceans* (1801), gives a good, detailed account
of the fur-trader's routes from Montreal to Winnipeg.   The
Reports of the Geological Survey of Canada also contain
much accurate information regarding the early trails and
portages of that region.

For the routes from the Great Lakes to the Mississippi,
Justin Winsor, *Mississippi Basin* (1895), and J. G. Shea,
Discovery and Exploration of the Mississippi (1853), in-
dicate authorities, and the *Jesuit Relations* (Thwaites'

ed., 1900) are full of indispensable information. Justin Winsor, *Cartier to Frontenac* (1894) and *Westward Movement* (1898), are also very useful, and F. A. Ogg, *The Opening of the Mississippi* (1904), is a recent work of value. Special studies of importance are E. J. Benton, *The Wabash Trade Route* (1903), G. A. Baker, *The St. Joseph-Kankakee Portage*, and F. H. Severance, *Old Trails on the Niagara Frontier* (2d ed., 1903). The histories of Parkman and others indicate many of the more important routes in the regions, with the special history of which they deal.

For the northern Appalachian routes, B. Willis, *The Northern Appalachians* (1895), is admirable. It is essentially a physiographic monograph, but considers historical relations and contains maps and diagrams. C. W. Hayes, *The Southern Appalachians* (1895), is a companion work to the preceding and is likewise excellent for the southern region. The majority of the important trails, portages, and passes of the east are dealt with in the numerous general histories of the colonies. For the south, besides the works of Hulbert, may be recommended T. Speed, *The Wilderness Road* (1886), and J. S. Johnston, *First Explorations of Kentucky* (1898). For the western routes the following works cover the ground: H. M. Chittenden, *The American Fur Trade of the Far West* (3 vols., 1902), a particularly good account of pioneer trading-posts in the Missouri Valley; E. Coues, *History of the Lewis and Clark Expedition* (4 vols., 1893), an authoritative account based on the journals of those explorers; H. Inman, *The Old Santa Fé Trail* (1897), a popular description of that route; J. C. Frémont, *Narrative of Exploring Expedition to the Rocky Mountains*, etc. (1846); W. H. Emory, *Notes of a Military Reconnaissance from Fort Leavenworth in Missouri to San Diego in California* (1848), an invaluable record of the work of the topographical engineers in their explorations in the Rocky Mountains and the southwest; and the historical works of H. H. Bancroft, *History of California* (7 vols., 1884–1890), *History of the Northwest*

Coast (2 vols., 1884), *History of Oregon* (2 vols., 1886–1888), and *Arizona and New Mexico* (1889). Francis Parkman, *Oregon Trail* (1872), is a fascinating account of the life along that route, and is fairly accurate.

TIMBER AND AGRICULTURAL PRODUCTS

As general descriptive works on the flora of the continent, the following are recommended: C. S. Sargent, *The Silva of North America* (14 vols., 1891–1902); E. Bruncken, *North American Forests and Forestry* (1900); N. L. Britton and A. Brown, *Illustrated Flora of the Northern United States and Canada* (3 vols., 1896); J. K. Small, *Flora of the Southeastern United States* (1903). These are all authoritative. On the economic relations and value of the various agricultural products the publications of the United States Department of Agriculture are the best sources of information. The *Year-Book* of the department, published annually since 1894, contains much condensed statistical information. The department also publishes special monographic studies from time to time, of which the following are notable: *The Cotton-Plant* (1896); C. Mohr, *The Timber Pines of the Southern United States* (1897); V. M. Spalding and B. E. Fernow, *The White Pine* (1899); H. W. Wiley, *The Sugar-Beet* (1899).

ANIMAL LIFE

On the distribution of the fauna, the two chief authorities are J. A. Allen and C. H. Merriam. The most important of their papers are: J. A. Allen, "The Geographical Distribution of North American Animals" (American Museum Natural History, *Bulletin*, 1892); C. H. Merriam, "The Geographic Distribution of Life in North America" (Biological Society, *Proceedings*, Washington, 1892); C. H. Merriam, "Laws of Temperature Control of the Geographic Distribution of Terrestrial Animals and Plants" (*National Geographical Magazine*, IV., 1894); J. A. Allen,

"The Geographic Origin and Distribution of North American Birds." (*The Auk*, 1893). Good general works on American natural history are few. W. Stone and W. E. Cram, *American Animals* (1902), limited to mammals in its subject matter, and the latest work, W. T. Hornaday, *The American Natural History* (1904), are the best in the field. Hornaday is particularly good on mammals, but not so strong on the other orders.

Of special studies, those on the bison and the fur-seal are the most important. J. A. Allen, "The American Bison, Living and Extinct" (Museum of Comparative Zoology, *Memoirs*, Cambridge, 1876), and W. T. Hornaday, "The Extermination of the American Bison" (National Museum, *Report*, 1889), contain most of the available information regarding the buffalo. David S. Jordan et al, *Report of the Fur-Seal Investigation* (4 vols., 1898), is a model of what such reports should be and is an exhaustive treatment of the whole subject. The best treatment of the deer is by Theodore Roosevelt and others, *The Deer Family*. The *Reports* of the United States Commission of Fish and Fisheries are recommended for information bearing on the economic value of the fisheries of the United States.

ARCHÆOLOGY OF NORTH AMERICA

The best bibliography of the extensive literature on this subject is that of Justin Winsor in his *Narrative and Critical History of America*, vol. I. (1889), excellent up to 1889. Another useful but uncritical bibliography is by G. Fowke in his *Archæological History of Ohio* (1902). The best general book on the subject is probably Cyrus Thomas, *Introduction to the Study of North American Archæology* (1898). H. W. Haynes, in Winsor, *Narrative and Critical History of America*, I., chap. vi., limits his discussion to the evidence as to man's antiquity. W. K. Moorehead, *Prehistoric Implements* (1900) is a good reference-book on the smaller objects which have been found.

The best publications on American archæology have

been monographs, and to the various writings of W. H. Holmes must be given the first place. These have appeared mainly under government auspices in Washington. The recent works of C. B. Moore on the mounds of Florida and the southeastern states are also model studies. These and other researches will be found noted in the special bibliographies mentioned above.

GENERAL WORKS ON THE INDIANS

There is no satisfactory comprehensive work on the American Indians. D. G. Brinton, *American Race* (1891), covers the tribes of both continents, but is so condensed that many groups of importance are not noticed and many points of fundamental significance are not even considered. While systematic in form the treatment is discursive and unsatisfactory. It is nevertheless a work of great learning and will be found useful by the student. T. Waitz, *Die Amerikaner*, in his *Anthropologie der Naturvölker*, pt. iii. (1862), is out of date, but still remains one of the best books on the subject. G. B. Grinnell, *Story of the Indian* (1896), is based on personal observations among the tribes of the west, but does not give a general survey. F. S. Dellenbaugh, *North Americans of Yesterday* (1901), is a pleasantly written, popular work, but is unsystematic in treatment. The author has, however, utilized the results of modern research. A good brief review is the article, "Indians," in the *New International Encyclopædia* (1904); and the articles in the same work on the individual tribes are, in general, excellent.

The older works which attempt to treat the subject in a general way are usually untrustworthy except where they relate to groups of which the authors had personal knowledge. The best-known books of this character are: J. Adair, *History of the American Indians* (1775), good for the southeastern tribes, but marred by certain absurd general theories; H. R. Schoolcraft, *His-*

torical and Statistical Information Respecting the History, Condition, and Prospects of the Indian Tribes of the United States (1851), and the same author's *American Indians* (1851), strongest for the Iroquois and eastern Algonquian Indians. G. Catlin, *Letters and Notes on the Manners, Customs, and Condition of the North American Indians* (1841), excellent for the tribes of the northern plains; J. L. McKenney and J. Hall, *History of the Indian Tribes of North America* (1836–1844); S. G. Drake, *Aboriginal Races of North America* (1860). Full references to the numerous other works of general scope will be found in Pilling, *Bibliographies*, noted below. For the last twenty-five years researches of great importance have been appearing, the bulk of which are contained in the *Annual Reports* of the Bureau of American Ethnology. This series will be found a storehouse of information on all subjects connected with the Indians, and while the value of the papers is very unequal they are in general well done. They will be referred to more in detail below.

INDIAN LINGUISTICS

The modern linguistic study of the Indians dates from the publications of Albert Gallatin issued at intervals from 1836 to 1853. A valuable bibliography of Gallatin and the authors who followed him in this field will be found in J.W. Powell, "Indian Linguistic Families" (Bureau of Ethnology, *Seventh Annual Report*, 1891). This paper of Powell's is the most important single publication on the subject which has yet appeared, its value resting largely on the linguistic map which accompanies it and which is reproduced in this volume. The best recent work on Indian languages has been done by A. S. Gatschet, J. O. Dorsey, and F. Boas, whose researches have been made chiefly under the auspices of the Bureau of Ethnology. Exhaustive linguistic bibliographies by J. C. Pilling have been issued by the same institution as follows: "Bibliography of the Eskimo Language" (*Bulletin*, 1887); "Bibliography of the Siouan Languages" (*Bulletin*, 1887); Bibliography of the Iroquoian Languages" (*Bulletin*, 1888); "Bibliography of the Muskhogean Languages" (*Bulletin*, 1889); "Bibliography of the Algonquian Languages" (*Bulletin*, 1891); "Bibliography of the Athapascan Languages" (*Bulletin*, 1892); "Bibliography of the Chinookan Languages" (*Bulletin*, 1893); "Bibliography of the Salishan Languages" (*Bulletin*, 1893); "Bibliography of the Wakashan Languages" (*Bulletin*, 1894). While Pilling's bibliographies are primarily linguistic, they include references to nearly all the early works of general description and are quite indispensable to the student.

THE ESKIMO

The best of the early accounts of the Eskimo is D. Cranz, *History of Greenland* (2 vols., 1767; 2d ed., 1820). The book is written from the point of view of the missionary, but contains much shrewd and accurate observation. The best later works are: E. Petitot, *Vocabulaire Francais-Esquimau* (1876); H. Rink, *Tales and Traditions of the Eskimo* (1876), *The Eskimo Tribes* (1887); F. Boas, "The Central Eskimo" (Bureau of Ethnology, *Sixth Annual Report*, 1888); J. Murdock, "Ethnological Results of the Point Barrow Expedition" (Bureau of Ethnology, *Ninth Annual Report*, 1892); E. W. Nelson, "The Eskimo about Bering Strait" (Bureau of Ethnology, *Eighteenth Annual Report*, 1899). A full bibliography up to 1887 will be found in Pilling, *Bibliography of the Eskimo Language*.

INDIANS OF THE NORTHWEST COAST

The literature on the North Pacific tribes has become quite extensive during recent years. This is largely due to the systematic observations which have been made by the British Association for the Advancement of Science. W. F. Tolmie and G. M. Dawson had previously published papers incidental to their geological work for the Canadian government, but the researches of F. Boas, under the auspices of the British Association, published in the *Reports* of that body (1885–1898), are the great sources of information. Other works of importance are: A. Krause, *Die Tlinkit Indianer* (1885); I. Petroff, *Report on the Population, etc., of Alaska* (1884); W. H. Dall, *Alaska and Its Resources* (1870); "The Distribution of Native Tribes of Alaska" (American Academy for the Advancement of Science, *Proceedings*, 1870); F. Boas, *Social Organization of the Kwakiutl Indians* (1897), *Indianische Sagen von der Nord-Pacif. Küste Amerikas* (1895); A. P. Niblack, "The Coast Indians," etc. (United States National Museum, *Report*, 1898).

INDIANS OF THE MACKENZIE RIVER BASIN

The literature on the Indians of the northern interior is scanty. The best authority is E. Petitot, whose works— *Grammaire comparée et Dictionnaire polyglotte des Dialectes Dènè-Dindjié* (1875), *Monographie des Dènè-Dindjié* (1875), *Ethnographie des Américains Hyperboréens* (1878), and *Traditions Indiennes du Canada Nordouest* (1886)—contain much accurate description. Father Morice, who has published papers in the *Transactions* of the Canadian Institute and in the *Proceedings* of the Royal Society of Canada, is also a good first-hand authority. Of the early descriptions, S. Hearne, *Journey from Prince of Wales Fort in Hudson Bay to the Northern Ocean* (1795), is the best. Sir A. Mackenzie, *Voyages from Montreal*, etc. (1801), should also be read.

INDIANS OF THE PLATEAUS

For the Salishan tribes, J. A. Teit, *The Thompson River Indians* (1898), is the best source of information. This is an exhaustive monograph based on personal observation, and is trustworthy. For the Shahaptian and neighboring stocks of the interior, the descriptions by

Meriwether Lewis and William Clark, contained in their
Journal, and the books which emanated from their expedition, are the sources of information with regard to the
early conditions.   P. J. de Smet, *Letters and Sketches*, etc.
(1843), and *Oregon Missions and Travels* (1847), are also
of value.   An excellent account of the distribution of the
tribes of the Columbia basin will be found in J. Mooney,
"The Ghost - Dance Religion" (Bureau of Ethnology,
Fourteenth Annual Report, 1896).

INDIANS OF WASHINGTON, OREGON, AND CALIFORNIA

The reports of F. Boas to the British Association for the
Advancement of Science, mentioned above, include ob-
servations on the Indians of the coast of Washington and
Oregon.   The same author's *Chinook Texts* (1894) also
contains general information of value.   J. G. Swan, "The
Indians of Cape Flattery" (Smithsonian Institution, *Con-
tributions to Knowledge*, 1869); M. Eels, "The Twana,
Chemakum, and Klallam Indians of Washington Territory"
(Smithsonian Institution, *Reports*, 1887); and G. Gibbs,
"Tribes of Western Washington and Northwestern Oregon"
(*Contributions to North American Ethnology*, 1887), are all
works of importance.   For the early condition of the
Chinook in the lower Columbia, the reports of the Lewis
and Clark expedition are the main sources.   A. S. Gatschet,
"The Klamath Indians of Southwestern Oregon (*Contributions to North American Ethnology*, 1890), is an excellent study of the Klamath and Modoc tribes.   Modern
research in California is all based on the classical
work of S. Powers, "Tribes of California" (*Contributions to North American Ethnology*, 1877).   H. H.
Bancroft, *The Native Races of the Pacific States* (5 vols.,
1874–1882), is also a standard work.   Two institutions—
the American Museum of Natural History and the Uni-
versity of California—are now carrying on systematic
researches among the Indians of California, and the
results are appearing in their regular publications.   At-

tention should also be called to the work of H. Hale on
the languages of the Pacific coast, in connection with the
United States Exploring Expedition under Wilkes, published in vol. VI. of the *Report* of that expedition (1846).

INDIANS OF THE GREAT PLAINS

The literature on this region is now extensive. The
best work on the Siouan family has been done by J. O.
Dorsey, whose most important papers are, "Omaha
Sociology" (Bureau of Ethnology, *Third Annual Report*,
1885), "The Cegiha Language" (*Contributions to North
American Ethnology*, 1892), "A Study of Siouan Cults"
(Bureau of Ethnology, *Eleventh Annual Report*, 1894), and
"Siouan Sociology" (Bureau of Ethnology, *Fifteenth
Annual Report*, 1897). A paper by J. Mooney, "The Siouan
Tribes of the East" (Bureau of Ethnology, *Bulletin*, 1894),
gives a full discussion of the evidence regarding the original
eastern habitat of the Sioux. Valuable reports have also
been published by S. R. Riggs, A. C. Fletcher, and others.
The best early authorities are Jonathan Carver, *Travels
through the Interior Parts of North America* (1778); George
Catlin, *Letters and Notes*, etc. (1841); and Prince Maxi-
milian zu Wied, *Travels in the Interior of North America*
(1843). An exhaustive bibliography up to 1887 will be
found in Pilling, *Bibliography of the Siouan Languages* (1887).

On the Blackfoot, consult H. Hale. "Report on the Black-
foot Tribes" (British Association for the Advancement of
Science, *Reports*, 1886); and for a popular account, G. B.
Grinnell, *Blackfoot Lodge Tales* (1903).

For the Pawnee or Caddoan family the available material
is slight. The early travels already mentioned give some
information; and of more modern work may be noted J.
B. Dunbar, in *Magazine of American History*, IV.,V.,VIII.;
G. B. Grinnell, *Pawnee Hero Stories and Folk Tales* (1889);
and several papers by A. C. Fletcher on Pawnee ceremonials
and myths, published in the *Journal of American Folk-
Lore*, *Reports of the Peabody Museum*, and under the auspices

of the Bureau of Ethnology. G. A. Dorsey is also publishing elaborate monographs on the myths and ceremonials, in the Field-Columbian Museum *Reports*. For the Kiowa the best information will be found in J. Mooney's admirable study, "The Calendar History of the Kiowa Indians" (Bureau of Ethnology, *Seventeenth Annual Report*, 1898).

ALGONQUIAN TRIBES

The bibliography of the Algonquian tribes is enormous. It will be found exhaustively treated in Pilling, *Bibliography of the Algonquian Languages* (1891). Of early works which may be especially recommended to the student are the *Jesuit Relations;* S. de Champlain, *Les Voyages de la Nouvelle France Occidentale* (1632); Jonathan Carver, *Travels*, etc. (1778); P. F. X. Charlevoix, *Histoire et Description Générale de la Nouvelle France* (1744); J. F. Lafitau, *Mœurs des Sauvages Amériquaines* (1724). Most of these deal primarily with the Iroquois but have much of interest regarding the Algonquian tribes of the northeast. The *Collections* of the Massachusetts Historical Society afford invaluable information regarding the New England tribes.

J. G. E. Heckewelder, *History of the Indian Nations Who Once Inhabited Pennsylvania and the Neighboring States* (1818; later ed., 1876), is the standard authority on the Delaware and contiguous tribes. Captain John Smith, *Generall Historie of Virginia* (1624), is the best early account of the southern tribes of the family.

For the Ojibwa, T. L. McKenney, *Sketches of a Tour of the Lakes* (1827); C. Atwater, *Indians of the Northwest* (1850); G. Copway, *Traditional History of the Ojibway Nation* (1850); and W. W. Warren, "History of the Ojibway" (Minnesota Historical Society, *Collections*, 1885), are recommended. W. J. Hoffman, "The Midewiwin, or 'Grand Medicine Society' of the Ojibwa" (Bureau of Ethnology, *Seventh Annual Report*, 1891), is excellent on the religious ceremonials of the tribe. For the central Algonquian tribes consult, in addition to the above, H. N. Beckwith, *The Illinois and Indiana Indians* (1884). This work covers particularly the historical period.

For the Iroquois, J. C. Pilling, *Bibliography of the Iroquoian Languages* (1888), should be consulted. Of the early writers, the *Jesuit Relations* and the descriptions of Lafitau, Charlevoix, and Champlain, mentioned above, as well as G. Sagard, *Le grand voyage du pays des Hurons* (1632), are the best. The most authoritative work is of later date. Cadwallader Colden, *History of the Five Indian Nations* (1727), and D. Cusick, *Sketches of Ancient History of the Six Nations* (1828), are two important early accounts of the league. Incomparably the most notable of all the researches on the Iroquois are the works of L. H. Morgan, of which *League of the Ho - dé - no - sau-nee, or Iroquois* (1851), "Systems of Consanguinity," etc. (Smithsonian Institution, *Contributions to Knowledge*, 1871), and *Ancient Society* (1877), are the chief. These are all masterly treatises; and, while many of Morgan's more general theories and conclusions cannot be accepted, he remains practically unassailed in his statements of facts.

H. Hale, *Iroquois Book of Rites* (1883), is also a scholarly piece of work and indispensable for the student. Both Morgan and Hale had the great advantage of intimate personal acquaintance with the Iroquois. W. M. Beauchamp has also published a number of papers of interest on the Iroquois, in the New York State Museum *Bulletins*. The introduction to F. Parkman, *The Jesuits in North America* (1867), gives a general discussion of the Indians with whom the Jesuits came in contact, and the whole book refers liberally and critically to the *Relations*. For the southern branch of the Iroquois family, the Cherokee, the monographs of C. C. Royce, "The Cherokee Nation of Indians" (Bureau of Ethnology, *Fifth Annual Report*, 1887), J. Mooney, "The Sacred Formulas of the Cherokee" (Bureau of Ethnology, *Seventh Annual Report*, 1891), "Myths of the Cherokee" (Bureau of Ethnology, *Nineteenth Annual Report*, 1900), cover the ground and refer to the sources.

The Muskhogean family in the southeast can best be studied through A. S. Gatschet, *Migration Legend of the Creek Indians* (1884), an excellent monograph with critical references to the sources. J. C. Pilling, *Bibliography of the Muskhogean Languages* (1889), is, of course, invaluable for the literature. Of the early writers, James Adair, *History of the American Indians* (1775), is based largely on personal observation and is the best known, but should be read with caution. C. MacCauley, "The Seminole Indians of Florida" (Bureau of Ethnology, *Fifth Annual Report*, 1887), describes the Florida Seminoles of to-day.

INDIANS OF THE SOUTHWEST AND MEXICO

The literature of this region is voluminous. A general discussion of the tribes, somewhat old but with many references to the early writers, is H. H. Bancroft, *The Native Races*, etc. (1874). For a general description of the Navajo, W. Matthews, *Navaho Legends* (1897), may be recommended. Special articles on the Navajo by the same writer will be found in the second, third, and fifth *Reports* of the Bureau of Ethnology. A study of "Navajo Houses," by C. Mindeleff (Bureau of Ethnology, *Seventeenth Annual Report*), should also be consulted. General popular works containing interesting descriptive matter are by G. W. James, *Indians of the Painted Desert Region* (1903); and G. A. Dorsey, *Indians of the Southwest* (1903). Neither of these works is critical.

For the Yuman stock, W. J. McGee, "The Seri Indians" (Bureau of Ethnology, *Seventeenth Annual Report*, 1898), may be noted. For the Pueblo group, A. F. Bandelier, "Final Report of Investigations among the Indians of the Southwestern United States" (Archæological Institute of America, *Papers*, 2 parts, 1890–1892), V. Mindeleff, "A Study of Pueblo Architecture" (Bureau of Ethnology, *Eighth Annual Report*, 1891), M. C. Stevenson, "The Sia" (Bureau of Ethnology, *Eleventh Annual Report*, 1894), and the various publications of F. H. Cushing and of J.

W. Fewkes, should be consulted. Cushing's studies on the Zuñi are especially brilliant, the best being "My Adventures in Zuñi" (*Century Magazine*, December, 1882, February, 1883, and May, 1883), "Zuñi Fetiches" (Bureau of Ethnology, *Second Annual Report*, 1883), "Pueblo Pottery as Illustrative of Zuñi Culture Growth" (Bureau of Ethnology, *Fourth Annual Report*, 1886), and "Outline of Zuñi Creation Myths" (Bureau of Ethnology, *Thirteenth Annual Report*, 1896). Fewkes's papers are careful and detailed, and refer particularly to the ceremonials. The following may be noted: "Provisional List of Annual Ceremonies at Walpi" (*Internationales Archiv für Ethnographie*, VIII., 1895), "Tusayan Katchinas" (Bureau of Ethnology, *Fifteenth Annual Report*, 1897), and a series of studies on Tusayan ceremonies, in the sixteenth and nineteenth *Annual Reports*, Bureau of Ethnology.

The Mexican literature can only be indicated. One of the best works on Mexican architecture is W. H. Holmes, "Archæological Studies among the Ancient Cities of Mexico" (Field-Columbian Museum, *Publications*, 1895–1897). On the general culture of the Aztec, A. F. Bandelier's epoch-making studies contain critical references to the sources and should be the starting-point of all work on that subject. They are: "On the Art of War and Mode of Warfare of the Ancient Mexicans" (Peabody Museum, *Tenth Annual Report*, 1877), "On the Distribution and Tenure of Lands, etc., among the Ancient Mexicans" (Peabody Museum, *Eleventh Annual Report*, 1878), and "On the Social Organization and Mode of Government of the Ancient Mexicans" (Peabody Museum, *Twelfth Annual Report*, 1880), *An Archæological Reconnoissance into Mexico* (no date); G. Brühl, *Die Cultur-völker Alt-Amerikas* (1875), will also be found useful.

INDIAN HOUSES, HOUSE-LIFE, AND THE FOOD QUEST

The information in this field is usually included in general descriptive studies. L. H. Morgan, "Houses and

House - Life of the American Aborigines" (*Contributions to North American Ethnology*, 1881), sums up the facts with regard to Indian dwellings as far as they were available at the time it was written. A general review will also be found in F. Ratzel, *History of Mankind*, II. (1897). Ratzel's treatment is not exhaustive and is unsatisfactory, but the work is very well illustrated.

The food quest is, of course, noticed in all the general works which have been mentioned. A. P. Jenks, "The Wild - Rice Gatherers of the Upper Lakes," etc. (Bureau of Ethnology, *Nineteenth Annual Report*, 1900), is a good study of a single phase of the subject. Indian economics is a problem much in need of special investigation.

INDIAN INDUSTRIAL LIFE

The best authority on this subject is O. T. Mason, and his books, *Woman's Share in Primitive Culture* (1894) and *The Origins of Invention* (1901), while not confined to America in their scope, are trustworthy and especially satisfactory in their treatment of the Indians. A number of studies by the same author, and by C. Rau and others, on special topics in this field, will be found in the publications of the Smithsonian Institution. F. S. Dellenbaugh, *The North Americans of Yesterday* (1901), also considers Indian industrial life at some length.

On pottery the numerous papers of W. H. Holmes, in the *Reports* of the Bureau of Ethnology, are the best; and on basketry, O. T. Mason, *Aboriginal American Basketry* (1904), is exhaustive and authoritative.

There is no good work on Indian warfare.

INDIAN SOCIAL ORGANIZATION

The chief authority on social organization is L. H. Morgan, whose *Ancient Society* (1877) is still the best work in the field. Morgan's other publications, *Houses and House-Life,* noticed above, and his *Systems of Consanguinity,* etc. (1871), also contain much information. For Mexico the works of A. F. Bandelier, already mentioned, are the best, and for the northwest the studies of F. Boas are the authorities. The general reader will find a remarkable condensation of the work of Morgan and Bandelier in the introduction to John Fiske, *Discovery of America* (1892). In his treatment of the Iroquois and Aztec, Fiske is judicious; but his more general views are open to much objection. Special studies of significance are J. W. Powell, "Wyandot Government" (Bureau of Ethnology, *First Annual Report*, 1881); J. O. Dorsey, "Omaha Sociology" (Bureau of Ethnology, *Third Annual Report*, 1884), and "Siouan Sociology," Bureau of Ethnology, *Fifteenth Annual Report*, 1897).

INDIAN RELIGION AND MYTHOLOGY

E. B. Tylor, *Primitive Culture* (2 vols., 1871), is the standard work on primitive religion, and is good in its treatment of American religious ideas. It also gives full references. The special studies on Indian religion are all in connection with inquiries bearing on mythology and ceremonials. D. G. Brinton, *Myths of the New World* (1868), and *American Hero Myths* (1882), are the only comprehensive works of value. They are dogmatic and untrustworthy, though learned. The American Folk-Lore Society, organized in 1888, publishes a *Journal* and a series of *Memoirs*, in which there is much material of great value. Several institutions, particularly the American Museum of Natural History and the Field-Columbian Museum, are also devoting attention to the collection of myths from special stocks, and the results may be found in their regular publications. Of the published collections, the following may be especially recommended: S. T. Rand, *Legends of the Micmacs* (1894); E. Petitot, *Traditions Indiennes du Canada Nord-Ouest* (1886); F. Boas, *Indianische Sagen* (1895); W. Matthews, *Navaho Legends* (1897); J. A. Teit, *Thompson River Indian*

Traditions (1898); and J. Mooney "Myths of the Cherokee" (Bureau of Ethnology, *Nineteenth Annual Report*, 1900).

Descriptions of ceremonials will be found in the works noted under special regions and in the publications of the Bureau of Ethnology, the American Museum of Natural History, and the Field-Columbian Museum. The literature is too extensive to be cited in detail.

On the practices of shamans, J. G. Bourke, "Medicine-Men of the Apache" (Bureau of Ethnology, *Ninth Annual Report*, 1892), will be found instructive; and on customs connected with death and burial, H. C. Yarrow, *Introduction to the Study of Mortuary Customs among the North American Indians* (1880), and "A Further Contribution to the Study of Mortuary Customs" (Bureau of Ethnology, *First Annual Report*, 1881) should be consulted.

INDIAN ART

There is no general review of Indian art. The best special studies are: F. W. Putnam, "Conventionalism in Ancient American Art" (Essex Institution, *Bulletin*, 1886); W. H. Holmes, "Origin and Development of Form and Ornament in Ceramic Art" (Bureau of Ethnology, *Fourth Annual Report*, 1886), "Study of Textile Art in Its Relation to the Development of Form and Ornament" (Bureau of Ethnology, *Sixth Annual Report*, 1888), also other papers by the same author in the *Reports* of the Bureau of Ethnology; F. Boas, "Decorative Art of the Indians of the North Pacific Coast" (American Museum of Natural History, *Bulletin*, IX., 1897); A. L. Kroeber, "Decorative Symbolism of the Arapaho" (*American Anthropologist*, III., 308, 1901).

INDEX

ABNAKI, Algonquian, 150.
Adaize family, 175.
Adoption custom, 204, 243.
Agriculture, fruits, 45; cereals, 46–50; sugar products, 50; hay, 51; cotton, 51; tobacco, 52; vegetables, 53; influence of products on national development, 53; Sioux, 135; Pawnee, 142; Algonquian, 151, 152; Pueblo, 184; Aztec, 213; Indian, 222, 223; bibliography, 275.
Algonquian family, tribes, 92; migrations, 98; plains tribes, 143, 144; seat, 148, 149; location of tribes, 149, 150; physique, 150; divergent culture, 151; agriculture, 152; houses, 152; social organization, 152; religion, mythology, 153; southern tribes, 163, 164; western tribes, 165; picture-writing, 165; present condition, 269; bibliography, 283.
Alligator, economic value, decrease, 67.
Animal life, wild, range, 54; relation with Eurasian fauna, 55–58; deer family, 58–61; sheep, 61; musk-ox, 62; buffalo, 62–64; fur-bearing animals, 65–67; animals valuable for hide, 67; birds, 67; fish, 68; Indian domestic 226; bibliography, 275, 276.

Antiquity of man. *See* Archæology.
Apache, Athapascan, culture, 181.
Apalache, Muskhogean, 167.
Appalachian system, extent and character, 9; Hudson River gap, 9; northern group, 9; central division, 9; central valley, 10; age, 14; portages over, 29; land routes over, 30–34.
Arapaho, plains Algonquian, 144.
Archæology, evidences of glacial man, 70; palæolithic remains, 71, 78; cave deposits, 73; status of mound-builders, 73, 81; distribution of remains, 73, 74; classification, 74; mounds, 75; enclosures, 76; hut-rings, 76; garden-beds, 77; quarries and workshops, 77, 78; copper-mining, 77; graves, 78; shell mounds, 78; comparative study, 79; ornaments, 79; stone objects, 80; human images, 80; weapons, 80; tools and utensils, 81; remains of Indian origin, 81, 85, 86; cliff-dwellings, 83; cave-dwellings, 84; pueblos, 84; Great Houses, 85; irrigation, 85; origin of man, 87; bibliography, 276.
Art, Eskimo, 107; of northwest coast tribes, 115; conven-